The Complete What UI
To Know

by Barry Maz

Copyright 2012 Barry Maz

To new ukulele players everywhere....

Cover photograph, Big Island Koa Concert Ukulele
– photo copyright Barry Maz 2012

CONTENTS

INTRODUCTION AND HOW TO GET THE MOST OUT OF THIS BOOK 1
1. HOW MUCH SHOULD I SPEND? 11
2. YES, BUT HOW CHEAP *IS* CHEAP? 17
3. THE HISTORY OF THE UKULELE 23
4. UKULELE SIZES 27
5. TUNING YOUR UKULELE 31
6. HOW TO HOLD AND STRUM THE UKULELE 37
7. HOW MUCH SHOULD I PRACTICE? 43
8. WHAT ARE THE 4 DIGIT NUMBERS I SEE FOR UKULELE CHORDS? 51
9. ALL THINGS STRINGS 55
10. HOW TO CHANGE UKULELE STRINGS 61
11. ALL ABOUT WOOD 67
12. MORE ABOUT WOOD 73
13. ALL ABOUT TUNING PEGS 79
14. CLEANING AND MAINTAINING YOUR UKULELE 83
15. ALL ABOUT NUTS AND SADDLES 91
16. INTONATION 95
17. SHOULD I PLAY WITH A PICK? 101

18. DEALING WITH BUZZES AND RATTLES. 103
19. HOW TO READ UKULELE TABLATURE (TABS) 111
20. SORE FINGERS? 117
21. UKULELE PICKUPS 121
22. FINGERNAILS 131
23. WHAT IS A K BRAND UKULELE? 135
24. ADVANCED STRUMMING TECHNIQUES 141
25. WHEN SHOULD I CHANGE MY STRINGS? 147
26. UKULELE WOODS AND THEIR INFLUENCE ON SOUND 151
27. DO I NEED A CASE? 157
28. FINGER STRETCHING EXERCISES 163
29. THE UKULELE BOOM 169
30. BASIC THEORY PT1 – NOTES 179
31. UKULELE ACTION 183
32. THE DREADED E CHORD 189
33. DEVICES TO TUNE YOUR UKULELE 195
34. LOW G TUNING AND RE-ENTRANT TUNING 201
35. BASIC THEORY PT2 – MAJOR CHORDS 207
36. UKULELE FINISHES 213
37. WHATS IN MY GIG BAG? 221

38. JAMMING, BUSKING AND PERFORMING 227
39. MUSICAL BARRIERS 239
40. BASIC THEORY PT3 – MINOR CHORDS. 243
41. MOVING FROM GUITAR TO UKULELE ... 247
42. STARTING A UKULELE CLUB 255
43. PORTABILITY IS THE THING 265
44. BASIC THEORY PT3 – 7th CHORDS 271
45. THE ALL INCLUSIVE UKULELE 275
46. HUMIDITY 281
47. MORE ADVANCED BUILDING TECHNIQUES 285
48. BUILDING A UKULELE WORKFLOW 291
49. MOVING ONWARDS 299
50. UKULELE INSPIRATION LIST 305
51. UKULELE REFERENCE 317
GLOSSARY 321
THANKS AND ACKNOWLEDGEMENTS 333
ALSO BY BARRY MAZ 337

INTRODUCTION AND HOW TO GET THE MOST OUT OF THIS BOOK

I'm Barry, and I'm a ukulele player. Well, actually, I am not just a player. In fact, I have found myself rather obsessed by the ukulele. You see, the little instrument can do that to you, it kind of gets under your skin. Before you know it, it has taken hold and you are stuck. It's fun though!

I actually started out in music as a guitar player and have been playing one of those for over twenty years, until a few years ago I was re-watching a documentary about a hero of mine, George Harrison. George liked the uke. In fact, that is an understatement, George LOVED the uke. In fact many of his friends are on record pointing out that he actually put the uke higher than the guitar in his affections. He would always travel with two or more ukuleles, so that if he was playing with friends, he could also pass one to somebody else to join in. I love that story. George had the ukulele bug bad, just like me. In fact, most people I meet who have started playing the ukulele have the same bug...

When I first bought a ukulele, totally contrary to all of my knowledge and good practice with guitars, I assumed the uke was a toy instrument, that it wasn't very serious. I therefore spent as little money as I could get away with in the hope of having some fun. How wrong I was. You see it turns out that the world is flooded with cheap ukuleles that frankly, don't play very well. Nor is the ukulele a toy or anything that shouldn't be taken seriously. It's an instrument and it needs the same thought and attention that any other instrument receives. This frustrated me, but I carried on, and bought a slightly better ukulele.

I then started to shop around for tuition books and resources on the web to help me. I started to notice a pattern. The tuition books were all very prescriptive – you MUST do this, you MUST play this way. The internet resources were not much better, and whilst the ukulele community out there in cyberspace is a very friendly one, I struggled to find concise answers to the most basic questions – the questions that just crop up. Sure, I could find a million sites to tell me how to play a G chord, or the chords to Daisy Daisy, but having been stung by a dodgy instrument I wanted to know more about owning a uke. It turns out there wasn't much out there directed at the absolute beginner. Nothing aimed at those people thinking about buying just to give it a go. So it crossed my mind, what percentage of those new players will take the route I took and buy a terrible instrument and become totally disillusioned with the uke? I worried that might be a high percentage.

So I put some effort into it, started to hone my ukulele playing skills, but this issue was still bugging me.

A few years ago I decided to bite the bullet and try to do something about it. I set up a blog called Got A Ukulele at http://gotaukulele.blogspot.com/. The aim of the blog was simple – it was to be a place for absolute beginners to visit to get answers to the questions they really needed answering before they chose to buy. It was to be a place that was never going to preach that you MUST do this or that, and it would deal with the simple stuff that troubles and tests every new musical instrument player. The blog did really well and is still being run with thousands of hits per day.

As part of that blog development, I started to put together rough beginners guides in one place, which became hugely popular. What you are reading now is an expanded collation of those beginners guides together with lots more information for reading wherever you may be. I have re-written many of the guides, and expanded them and hope this book provides just the resource, all in one place, that I so hoped to find when I started with the ukulele. This book collects the guides provided in my first two books in one place. The books have been called 'owners manuals for new ukulele players' and I like that!

I look upon my decision to play the ukulele as one of the best decisions I ever made. It is a happy instrument. I have never yet played it in public without people smiling and nodding in appreciation. It is a perfect 'pick me up' when I am down. It's a friend, it's a great way of killing time but it is also a challenge. It' a social instrument and I have made many new friends playing it too.

So here you have what I like to think is a no-nonsense set of guides for new ukulele players. I don't want to preach, just advise. You may, in time, find better techniques – let me know about them and share your thoughts. Most of all though, I hope that if you read this book before you start playing, when you hit your first hurdle (and believe me, you will!), that you decide to carry on and break through it.

Keep strumming!

How to make best use of this book

This book is intended to become a companion piece to carry with you when you cannot access the Got A Ukulele website, or just a good read – either way I hope it helps you out. A depository, if you will, of knowledge that you might need wherever you are. I have also added a glossary and reference section for you to explore further. I would like to think that if you are an absolute beginner, after reading this book you will feel more confident about learning, buying and just living with a ukulele in your life. That is the whole point of it.

Despite my concerns about the prescriptive nature of the tuition books out there, I suggest you read this book in conjunction with them. I say that for the simple reason that this book format is not the best for me to provide chord boxes, photographs and sheet music. As such I suggest you get a few songbooks and a basic tuition book too. Read those in conjunction with my guides, and keep in mind that you don't HAVE to do things a certain way just because Bob the Ukulele Tutor says so in his book (sorry Bob, whoever you are..). I have included a bit of basic theory in the latter chapters of the book to start you off, but this book is not meant to replace proper theory and tuition.

Before reading further I would urge you to visit the Got A Ukulele site and download and print the various chord sheets that are on that site (they are free!). You will need them for understanding certain chapters of this book. Print them off and slip them in your ukulele case so you know where they are. As a beginner you should always have a chord chart with you! Alternatively, if you prefer the ebook revolution, I have a ukulele chord book available online for most ereaders called Chords That Ukulele Players Really Want To Know.

If you have bought your ukulele already, then I suggest you also print off some simple songs that you enjoy (two or three chord songs) and invest in a functional ukulele tuner. It will mean less tears at bedtime...

This second half of this book comes from my second volume and takes a slightly different angle to the first half in many ways. By the time you have reached those chapters it may be helpful for you to have mastered the basics of strumming and the ability to get yourself through a few songs. You may find that one or two other things are then bugging you, or that you find yourself thinking about the ukulele and wanting to do more with it. The later chapters provides more beginner tips on various elements of ukulele ownership and playing, but it also includes some more general thoughts and advice that may assist in your life with a ukulele and moving forward with it. In that respect I hope some of the chapters in this book inspire as well as inform.

I owe a huge amount of thanks to those who have supported Got A Ukulele over the years – it is hugely enjoyable to be involved with and I have got to know a large number of wonderful ukulele people along the way. Thanks to some of those are included at the end of the book.

Finally, have a look at the final chapters of this book that contain a helpful glossary and a list of useful ukulele resources that I think you should be aware of. Make yourself aware of the various terminology associated with the uke. Have a look at the resources, join an Internet forum or two and don't be afraid to ask questions. The uke community likes to help!

As I say to everyone who reads my blog, feedback is positively encouraged, and I would urge you always to get in touch via bazmazwave@gmail.com with any suggestions or if you need any more advice. I am always happy to help!

Enjoy and keep strumming!

Barry

1. HOW MUCH SHOULD I SPEND?

Okay, you are saying, you have convinced me, I'm going to give the ukulele a try, but how much do I need to spend? Are these things expensive, and do I have to spend half of my yearly wage just to get one?

This is a very common question and really, the answer depends on your personal circumstances. Even so, unless you are 'Mr Moneybags', there is little point in spending many hundreds on a first ukulele only to find you don't enjoy it. (Well, I suppose it could make a nice wall decoration, but you know what I mean).

At the other end of the scale, whilst it obviously seems tempting to spend as absolutely little as possible, (as you are just testing the ukulele waters!), you should also be careful not to be too cheap. As with guitars, if you purchase something so cheap that it is badly made, you will find the instrument working against you from the start. Learning a stringed instrument for the very first time does take some practice and time. Purchase a super cheap ukulele that is impossible to tune or has an unplayable set-up (the term used to describe the set up of the adjustable parts of the ukulele providing a good playing experience) and you are just adding to the difficulty unnecessarily. In the worst case this could put you off forever, which would be a shame, as you don't need to spend a lot to get a playable instrument.

If, like many of us do, you use eBay, do a search for "ukulele" and you will find a range of instruments in super-bright colours for anything from £10 to £20. My advice is DON'T!. I've sampled instruments at this low end with brand names that sound suitably Hawaiian, and in many, many cases they are seriously badly made. I'm not just talking about finish or the paintwork, they can just be so badly made that they will make tuning, set-up and playing extremely difficult indeed. There may be some good ones in there, but if budgets are tight, why take the risk?

I would consider going no lower than around £30 for a first instrument, and would highly recommend the Makala range of ukuleles, particularly the Dolphin model. The Dolphin is a remarkable instrument, which when fitted with good quality strings is remarkably loud, accurate and sweet sounding. I own a Makala Dolphin and have actually performed live with one! Avoid trying to shop around with Dolphins to save a a few pennies from a random eBay seller- Dolphins need a small amount of set-up to sound their best, so buy from a store who will set up for you. If you are not sure, call them and ask the question. If they are a good dealer, they will do this for you. If they refuse, I would move on.

Moving up into the £30 to £60 range and you are still looking at the Makala range of instruments being your best option in my opinion. In the £60 plus region look for instruments made by Lanikai, I have owned one and they are superb beginner instruments with a very good sound, particularly the LU21 model.

As you rise above the £60 mark you start to find your choice of instrument starts to widen dramatically. Of note in this range are ukuleles from Kala and Ohana. These are very good (and nice looking) instruments made in the Far East.

Up to this point we are talking about laminate ukuleles only. This means that the wood is not solid wood, but really a plywood (more on that later in the book) Laminate instruments are generally not as sweet sounding as solid wood models, but for a beginner they are just fine.

If you absolutely must have a solid wood instrument, about the cheapest you will find are the entry-level models from Bruko. These are (amazingly) handmade in Germany, are made completely from solid wood, and start at around £100.

If you intend to purchase your first ukulele above the £100 mark, things start to become complicated as the range becomes huge. Sadly there are still plenty of 'bad eggs' so how do you know where to go? Well if you are paying this much, I would definitely recommend that you try to play before you buy to check that the instrument works for you. This money is considered by many to be a serious amount for a ukulele so you really should be careful. If that isn't possible, I would recommend that you do your best to 'play safe'.

The safest option I can recommend is to buy a Flea ukulele made by the Magic Fluke Company. They are, due to their construction, almost guaranteed to be set up well. This is an important consideration for the new player, as this will leave you with very little to worry about other than practising your new instrument. Ohana and Kala instruments in this range are very good instruments too, but I don't think they are likely to be as consistent as the Flea and would recommend you try to play them first. Fleas can be found for around £140. in the UK.

If you can push on towards £200 mark I would, without any doubt urge you to look at a Mainland ukulele. They are widely considered to be about the best value all solid instruments you can buy and they sound superb. Set up is always spot on and they look great too! You can probably find a starter Mainland for around £180.

Beyond that you are on your own! Choose very carefully, avoid the bargain basement and read the ukulele forums thoroughly. They are full of friendly people happy to help. I wish you good luck in the purchase of your new ukulele!

2. YES, BUT HOW CHEAP *IS* CHEAP?

I thought that to supplement my guide on what to spend on a ukulele that I would give you some first hand advice as to the path that I actually took in starting to play the uke. I made some mistakes.

Generally speaking, buying a ukulele is like buying any other musical instrument. Go too cheap and you will end up with something that may hinder your learning and put you off. This is not a good thing, and don't convince yourself that you will be able to 'manage'. A badly made instrument may not be capable of being tuned properly, and a poor set-up is not only difficult to play but could also cause you to develop some bad playing habits as you try to compensate.

I fully appreciate that for many people, lots of money is just not available, and they certainly don't have never ending funds to blow on a musical instrument that they are not even sure they will enjoy playing. Heck, ukuleles can cost more than

£500, but how low CAN you go?

A quick search of eBay will show a variety of brightly coloured instruments in the £15 - £20 range. Do beware. I bought one of these and it was really good for nothing more than plywood. The first one I bought had two frets set at an angle, which meant accurate playing was a complete impossibility.

Step up a level into the £25 - £50 range, and you are in to the level that I would recommend for beginners. Bear in mind that these entry ukuleles won't be solid, and will definitely benefit from changing strings (so budget another £6 or so). They may also need a tweak to set up such as slight lowering of the action. This will be a breeze if you are a guitar nut, but newcomers will need to bear in mind that if the dealer won't do this for you, you may need to consider paying a luthier or guitar technician to do this for you.

Moving up into the £50 - £100 bracket and you start to find more improvements in quality, and some solid woods. This is, however, the category to take the most care with. We are getting into more serious money now, and, sadly, there are more bad instruments here that shouldn't in my view command these higher prices. Look out for Kala, Lanikai, and Ohana. If you can reach £100, check out entry level Bruko instruments. All ukuleles in this range may still need action checking and may benefit from better strings.

Up a step again into the £100 - £200 category and your choice widens considerably. I think this is the range where you really can get ALL the uke you need without going for a boutique or handmade instrument. All of my own first upper end instruments were in this range. Wooden ukuleles will tend to be ALL solid in this range (or at least solid topped), and whilst still made in Asia may be finished in USA, such as the brilliant Mainlands. Very nice Kala and Ohana instruments can be found in this range too, as well as the standard model Fleas and Flukes (everyone should own one! USA made)

Higher still and it's a case if 'where do you stop'? You are looking at upgraded versions of the above in exotic woods, or with pickups fitted, or into the range beautiful hand made Hawaiian and luthier built instruments!

So, what did I do? That's what you really want to know!

Ukulele 1 – Mahalo for just under £20 – a horrible, horrible instrument, so badly put together that the frets were noticeably fitted at an angle making tuning impossible. Mahalo may well have improved since but I will never forget this instrument.

Ukulele 2 - Vintage – About £25, and needed quite a lot of work to make it play properly. Sound is very thin, but it was playable.

Ukulele 3 - Lanikai - £55 – a very nice sounding ukulele that needed only minimal setting up and sounds rather nice, if a little thin.

Ukulele 4 -Flea = £120 – My first foray into

purchasing a 'proper' ukulele – when I first took this instrument out, the first thing that surprised me was that despite it being shipped from one end of the country to the other, it was still in tune. The instrument is so rock solid and so well made that it really is idiot proof. Playing it was sublime compared to my other instruments, instantly relegating them to the cupboard under the stairs.

Ukulele 5 - Mainland - £160 – my second 'proper' ukulele which is just as much of a joy to play as the Flea due to its impeccable set-up and construction. This balances my Flea nicely as it has a warmer sound.

Having bought all of those ukuleles, I then invested in several more and now have quite a collection. The real marvel though was the purchase of my first Makala Dolphin for one of my children. For the price of only £30, I was staggered at how well made the instrument was and how good it sounded. Not quite as nice as my Flea, but really, not far off, and significantly nicer than any of my earlier ukuleles. I like them so much I now own three of them, and leave one in the boot of my car so I always have a ukulele with me!

3. THE HISTORY OF THE UKULELE

So, where does the ukulele come from? Many people assume it originated in Hawaii, but is that really true? Read on!

The ukulele is commonly associated with music from Hawaii where the name roughly translates as "jumping flea", due to the action of one's fingers playing the ukulele resembling a "jumping flea". According to Queen Lili'uokalani, the last Hawaiian monarch, the name means "the gift that came here", from the Hawaiian words uku (gift or reward) and lele (to come). Developed in the 1880s, the ukulele is based on a small guitar-like instrument, the machete (similar to, though smaller than, the modern Portuguese cavaquinho and the Spanish timple), introduced to the Hawaiian Islands by Macaronesian (Portuguese and Spanish) immigrants. Three immigrants in particular, Madeiran cabinet makers Manuel Nunes, José do Espírito Santo, and Augusto Dias, are generally credited as the first ukulele makers. Two weeks after they landed aboard the Ravenscrag in late August 1879, the Hawaiian Gazette reported that "Madeira Islanders recently arrived here, have been delighting the people with nightly street concerts." One of the most important factors in establishing the ukulele in Hawaiian music and culture was the ardent support and promotion of the instrument by King David Kalakaua. A patron of the arts, he incorporated it into performances at royal gatherings.

So, it's actually Portugese in origin, but that said, the ukulele will always, understandably be rooted in Hawaiian culture.

Since it's arrival in Hawaii, it really hit boom time at the turn of the 20th century becoming a staple instrument of variety acts in the US and the UK, with Cliff Edwards and George Formby respectively promoting the instrument either side of the Atlantic.

It then fell out of favour, but has seen an amazing resurgence in the last 10 years. I suspect that Mr Formby would have been staggered to see just how wide ranging the ukulele now is in popular music, played and loved by everyone from folkies to punks, metal fans to the traditional Hawaiian musicians.

As a foot note to this short chapter, the Hawaiian connection does provide us with a possible answer to a common question – how do you pronounce the word UKULELE.

Well, the Hawaiian pronunciation of the word is OOK-KAH-LAY-LEE. That said, on this side of the pond, we tend to use YOOK-AH-LAY-LEE. Who is right? It's further complicated by the fact the far more common pronunciation of the short form of the word UKE is YOOK, and not OOK (though some people say it that way). Does it matter? Not really, the thing is for playing not naming!

4. UKULELE SIZES

Size does matter!

If you are a beginner to ukulele, you may find further confusion when you see the different sizes of uke. They start from the super small to instruments that are not far off the size of a guitar. But which is which, and which do you want?

Generally speaking, the smaller the uke, the more of a 'uke' sound I think it has - a shriller sound if you like. As you move up the sizes, as well as increases in the volume of your sound, you will also get a fuller thicker sound (and more bass!)

The sizes are often linked to their "scale length". That means the length between nut (the white strip the strings rest on at the tuning end of the ukulele) and bridge (the white strips the strings run over on the top of the body), an is a gauge of both the size of the instrument generally, but also the amount of notes you can play on the neck (quite simply as a longer neck allows for more frets, and therefore a wider range of notes)

The standard sizes of ukulele are:

Soprano (or standard)

Approximate 13" scale length - the little baby uke and the most traditional. Great for a beginner, though some with larger hands may find the fret spacing a little small. Also, a limited number of frets can limit some high notes for playing fancier tunes. Usually tuned GCEA (C tuning) with a high G-string, though other variants exist such as ADF#B (D tuning).

Concert

Approximate scale length 15" - slightly larger body

gives more volume and warmth to the sound. Longer scale allows for more frets, and more comfortable spacing for fat fingers! This is quickly becoming the best-recommended ukulele for a beginner – very easy to play, but still obviously "uke looking"! Concert ukuleles are usually tuned GCEA with a high G (ie the G string is above the C string in pitch not below it), but larger concerts work well with a low G.

Tenor

Approximate scale length 17" - bigger again, with a fuller sound - tuned usually low GCEA or DGBE

Baritone

Approx scale length 19" - the big daddy - usually tuned DGBE and approaching the size of a small guitar.

That's the basics of it – the instrument you choose

depends on where you want the instrument to fit in with your band or set up. If you are just looking to start to play the uke for fun, and have never played before I would personally suggest trying to obtain a concert scale model, though a soprano will be just fine.

There are other complications (such as Sopranino sizes, Sopranos with concert necks, five and six string ukes, resonators and banjoleles etc) but that would be for another chapter altogether!

5. TUNING YOUR UKULELE

Well, first things, first. Your new ukulele has arrived in the post and you want to start playing it. It is extremely unlikely that your instrument is properly in tune. Even if it was tuned at the shop, new ukulele strings have a horrible habit of stretching and stretching, so you need to be prepared to do a lot of ukulele tuning in the first few weeks! So, grab your tuner of choice (see below) and let's begin.

There are a variety of ways to tune a soprano ukulele, and to go through them all would defeat the purpose of this book (i.e. beginner basics). I am therefore looking at standard tuning in the key of C, by far the most common way to tune a Soprano, and most ukuleles.

First, some basics for you. On your instrument you have four strings. As you hold your ukulele the string nearest the floor is string 1. The string nearest your face (or the ceiling) is string 4. You can work out which are strings 2 and 3 yourself.... Quite why they are not numbered the other way around I really don't know because it would seem to make sense to me for them to be numbered top to bottom, not bottom to top. Oh well, that is the convention, and you need to remember it as you will need it for reading chords, tabs and whenever you next string your instrument.

The C tuning uses the following notes, running from the bass (face/ceiling) end to the treble (ground end) of the sequence of GCEA.

In other words, the strings are tuned like this

String 4 - G
String 3 - C
String 2 - E
String 1 - A

(that 4th string can be tuned a low G or a high G, that is to say, low being the G below the C on string 3 or the G that is naturally above the C on string 3).

On a soprano ukulele, a high G is much more common (meaning it is higher than most of the other strings), but as you move up uke sizes, you may consider a low G. Remember though, it is just a case of sound – a G is a G is a G, they are just an octave apart.

To tune your instrument, you need some sort of reference pitch to work from. If you are a super natural, you may tune from your ear (good luck to you, I cant... I'm jealous; I'll get over it...). Other than that, the next step I suppose is tuning from a piano, another instrument or tuning forks in the notes you need.

However, to be honest with you, in this day and age, if you are spending some money on a ukulele, and you are a beginner - buy yourself a clip on tuner. They are about £10-£20 and clip onto the headstock of the instrument and magically help you tune. There are all sorts of varieties out there, and if you want flexibility look for one that works on both vibration and sound (though that isn't essential). They work by picking up the sound of the instrument (or the vibrations) and display a handy LED needle that turns green when your tuning is spot on. Failing that, a Google search for 'online ukulele tuner' will throw up lots of results for sites that will give you a good reference pitch. If you use an iPhone, there are also plenty of free programs in the App Store.

So, whatever your method, pluck the string clearly, check with your reference or tuner – if you are flat (i.e. lower than the note you need) then tighten the tuning peg. If you are sharp (higher) then loosen the string. Job done.

Hang on – is that it? Well, really, yes – the tuners only work in two ways, and when you are in tune you are in tune. I suppose there is a little more to it than that though. For example, it is good practice to tune UP to pitch. In other words, if you are tuning and your string is high (sharp) loosen it a little until it is lower (flatter) than the note you require and tune up from there. This helps to ensure strings don't slip and that the tuning pegs are under tension. Don't be tempted to over tune the string and then just knock it back a little on the peg – that is bad practice.

Also, as I said above, if you are adding a new string, or a new set, they will need time to stretch and settle. I personally give them a shove in the right direction by stretching them by hand. Once on and tuned to the right note - put your forefinger under the string at its halfway point, and pull up and away from the neck of the instrument about half of an inch or so (not too hard, it's not a archery bow!!) then check the tuning again - it will most likely be flat. Tune again to the correct pitch and repeat until the stretching makes very little difference to your tuning. At this point your strings are pretty much where you want them though you may find some more small stretching over the next few days, but nothing too much. If you don't like the idea of manual stretching, just keep re-tuning your instrument day by day, but be aware that they could take a week or two to finally settle down. That is normal and it doesn't mean there is something wrong with your instrument!

The best tips I can give though – use good strings, use a clip on tuner and take care with your tuning. If the uke sounds bad – check that tuning and carry on playing.

6. HOW TO HOLD AND STRUM THE UKULELE

A very obvious question asked by ukulele beginners is how to hold and strum the thing! On the face of it you would think that it's really rather simple – you hold it against your chest, strum with one hand and fret with the other. Well, yes, that's it basically, but I actually find that ukulele guidebooks can be far too prescriptive. The ukulele is an instrument that you need to be at one with, so most importantly YOU need to be happy with the way you are playing it.

As with most things musical instrument related, you will find a lot of resources out there that tell you that you MUST do this or that. Usually they are wrong, and miss the very important point of letting you do what you are happy and comfortable with. Of course, a very bad habit can work against you, but generally speaking I find that with ukuleles as with guitars, you have an amount of freedom. Look at it this way - did Jimi Hendrix play his guitar in the same way as a Spanish flamenco player? No. They are both guitars, but they have different styles. It's the same with ukes, and you need to find your own style too.

HOLDING THE UKE

The ukulele is designed to be held by the strumming arm, pressed lightly against the chest. They are not particularly heavy, and by placing the uke against the chest you should find that you are able to hold the uke steadily by pressing the the top of the uke (see the Glossary, the top is the name given to the flat top of the instrument with the sound hole in it) below the sound hole against your chest with the inside of the bicep of the strumming arm.

That is not a hard and fast rule. Some people prefer to play sitting down and rest the uke on their knee - that's good too. If you want to stand but struggle with holding the ukulele, you can resort to a strap or support like the UKE LEASH which I favour.

Do what feels right to you! So long as you have the instrument in a position where you are free to move both your fretting hand and your strumming hand, and in a way that you are not muffling the sound or squeezing the uke too hard, then you are good to go. Play it behind your head if you like (see, I thought the Jimi Hendrix reference would work well....)

STRUMMING THE UKE

The conventional method for strumming the ukulele is to use the fingers (not a pick) of the strumming hand. The traditional style is to only move the wrist keeping the forearm fixed (and holding the uke). You need to strum over what we call the "sweet spot" which is usually at the end of the fingerboard in front of the sound hole (note - this is the opposite of the sweet spot for an acoustic guitar which is normally strummed behind the soundhole). Try strumming your instrument in a variety of positions down from the end of the neck, moving towards the sound hole. You will find the spot that both feels and sounds just right. The conventional thinking is that strumming at the end of the fingerboard means there is less chance of fingers getting tangled in the strings. Whilst this is probably true for beginners, a seasoned ukulele player will be able to strum anywhere without getting tangled, and I am of the view that it is recommended to strum there because you will find the best sound.

Again, that is not a hard and fast rule. I have what you may call an 'unusual' uke strumming style (check out my videos on the Got A Ukulele blog) as I tend to lightly rest the fleshy part of the side of my hand (thumb side) just above the sound hole, and strum with my forefinger downwards. I can strum in the conventional way, but I just find this more comfortable to me. Let's not fall out about it...

Some folks will rely just on their thumb to strum (a very laid back style) or use a pick. Again it is all good.

If you are just starting out, you will read lots about

strum styles and patterns, fans and triplets. Honestly, this is more advanced technique than you need right now - just concentrate on getting the ukulele in a position you like, and a strum that you can do effortlessly and in good rhythm before worrying about fancy strum patterns.

YouTube is your best resource for seeing people play - do a search for ukulele and have a look at the many different ways people hold and strum the ukulele

Find what works for you!

7. HOW MUCH SHOULD I PRACTICE?

This is a very difficult question to answer, but one I get asked a lot, in fact perhaps the most - how much should one practice ukulele, and how much is too much (if that's possible)

I don't know whether we will get to the bottom of that answer, but I hope this chapter talks around the subject enough to give you comfort if you are confused or concerned.

First off, whilst you will read a lot on the web about how easy the ukulele is, it's important to understand that the statement is relative. For an absolute beginner, no instrument is particularly easy to learn (well, perhaps maracas or a triangle..), and stringed instruments present their own problems in terms of finger tip pain and the need to build up strength and flexibility. With the ukulele, you WILL be able to strum a basic song very very quickly, and I do often boast that I could get somebody playing a 2 chord song in half an hour. That is NOT the ukulele mastered though - that can take a lifetime, and that only comes with practice.

The important thing to learn if you are starting out, or perhaps thinking of purchasing for a son or daughter - PRACTICE IS THE ABSOLUTE KEY. It really is. There are no short cuts, no special tips or accelerated programmes to leaning the ukulele - like so many things, it takes hard work, dedication and effort. You will therefore have to practice, and regular practice is best.

How *much* to practice? - well that depends on your mindset, how quickly you want to learn, and what level you are at now. A beginner may well need to sink more hours into practice than, say, and accomplished player will want to in order to keep on top of their game. Certainly an hour or half an hour a day would be great, more if you have the time. Ten minutes each weekend will, I suspect, make your progress SO slow, that you will probably get frustrated and potentially give up, and we really don't want that do we? (You've only just started this book!!)

How much practice is too much? That's a really hard one to answer. Is it possible to practice too much? Can it do you any harm? Will the sky fall in? I would personally suggest you are practicing too much if:

- You are not enjoying it any more
- You are not noticing any improvement between sessions
- You are in serious pain

I actually think the first bullet point is the most serious, as too much as pain is a worry to anyone. Push anything to the point it becomes a chore and no fun any more and you risk doing so much damage to your attitude and passion that it may not recover. You need, however, to watch the signs - many beginners don't enjoy practice out of frustration, and they need to break through a wall – that's perfectly normal and understandable, don't give up too early. If you are noticing any of the above, I would suggest you take a short break of a day or two, then consider practicing for shorter periods or slightly less often. As you become more accomplished you will find that you naturally find your own balance for practice (and you have less risk of your significant other packing your bags and asking you to leave the house).

So keep at it - don't be daunted - you WILL break through, and suddenly you will see your ability grow quicker - believe me, it is worth it.

My tips for absolute beginners starting out:

- Download the free chord chart from the Got A Ukulele website - don't be daunted. Start off by ensuring you know at least a handful of the most common chords. Common chords are those that appear mostly in the songs YOU want to learn, but I would say A, Am, Bm, C, C7, D, D7, Em, F, G, G7 to start with. Make sure you know them immediately someone shouts one out and you can move your fingers to the chord cleanly. Try to remember what they sound like, and what they look like on the fingerboard. Don't try and learn every one in your first session, pick two and work on them until they are etched in your brain, then move on to the others. Knowing a good handful of chords is key to developing with the uke.

- Practice your strumming technique and find the posture and approach that FEELS right to you. There is no right and wrong. I dislike sites that provide songs with the exact up and down stroke notation for when to strum - you need to learn to feel the rhythm of the song you are attempting and find your own style (unless you want to copy it parrot fashion, but that's no fun in my eyes).

- Try to start with some songs that have a clear chugging rhythm that is easy to get into – avoid anything with complicated timing, or that go at the speed of sound. As silly as it sounds, Nursery Rhymes are great for practice as most people know them by heart and they are simple. Most of all choose some songs that YOU enjoy playing and already know quite well. This will make it more fun.

• When you have the chords mastered, ensure that you can switch back and forth between ANY of them instantly and at will. Practice some chord patterns (make them up) and notice which patterns sound good together, and which ones don't. You are now starting to understand what makes music work.

• Whilst doing all of the above, have a few simple three chord song sheets on hand to use for practice - don't limit your practice just to technique or desperately trying to master the latest chart hit that you like - you will progress quicker if you do some drill. Spend the start of your practice session on the boring stuff (testing yourself on your chords, changes, notes etc.), then the second half on a song you like as a treat.

Beyond the above, you will become an actual player soon. You can then start to worry about more exotic chords, palm muting the strings, learning scales and finger picking, but don't worry about any of those just yet - nail the basics.

Most importantly - KEEP AT IT!

8. WHAT ARE THE 4 DIGIT NUMBERS I SEE FOR UKULELE CHORDS?

A common question that probably confuses absolute ukulele beginners - what are the four digit numbers that people print when talking about ukulele chords?

Well this is just a simple form of notation for a ukulele chord without drawing a ukulele chord box and showing with a drawing where the fingers go. It's really very simple and worth understanding as you wont always see the chord boxes when finding songs to play.

To help explain, grab the ukulele chord sheet you printed from the Got A Ukulele website (you did read the introduction didn't you??) and read on.

Looking at the top chord chart (standard tuning for soprano in GCEA), lets look at the first chord box on the top line, the C chord. To play that chord, the chord box is showing you the string nearest your face /ceiling (string 4) on the far left, and the string nearest the floor (string 1) on the far right. We have a black spot on the A string (the one nearest the floor) at the third fret position (the third gap down from the top). This is the only note that is fretted for this particular chord, and the rest are played open (meaning that they are strummed without touching them with your fretting hand). If you strum this you get a C. Now, without a chord box, how do we express that? Well the notation in 4 digits is 0003. A zero means the string is played open, and of course the 3 means you hold that bottom string at the third.

Lets try another one. Turn to sheet two of the standard soprano tuning sheet to the second sheet and find the standard G chord (first one, second row down). The diagram is telling you to play the G string open, the C string at the 2nd fret, the E string at the 3rd fret and the A string at the 2nd fret. In digit notation, that would be written 0232. Simple eh?

Have a look at the other chord boxes and see if you can work some others out. To test you, what do the following digit notations represent (using the soprano GCEA chord charts)

0202
2100
4322

Did you work them out?

A further marking in the 4-digit notation you may see, is where the notation requires you to mute or ignore playing a string. To play the G chord without hitting that G-string, you would write this as X232 (The cross indicating that string is not to be played).

It is important to follow this, as on the many friendly ukulele forums and groups you will often see chords expressed this way. It's also extremely handy when you are playing with others as you can quickly tell another player how to play the chord you are on by simply yelling a four-digit number.

9. ALL THINGS STRINGS

Rather like guitar, there is a range of strings available for the ukulele. If you are a ukulele beginner and have bought an entry-level instrument, the chances are, it will arrive with very cheap basic strings on it. You can tell, they will be jet black and shiny, or clear and shiny. They are usually nothing more than cheap fishing line or twine and will do nothing to help you pull a nice tone and volume out of your instrument.

One of the very best (and simplest) upgrades you can make to a cheaper ukulele is a string upgrade - probably costing you no more than about £6 or £7. (Six or seven pounds? I hear you cry, but my ukulele only cost me twenty – that's ridiculous!! - It isn't – those very cheap ukuleles are cheap for a reason, and the strings are only worth pennies. Trust me!). If you are sat with your new uke and have those slippy nasty black strings that it arrived with on it, please, please, consider a string change.

Now, don't expect to walk into your local music shop and see a huge range of ukulele strings, that just isn't going to happen unless you are lucky to have a local store with impeccable taste... This is, however, where eBay or the Internet is your friend. Do a search and you will find a big range.

The two sets of strings that I heartily recommend are the following:

Aquila

Italian made strings, from a substance called nylgut, which attempts to recreate the properties of real gut that instruments used to be strung with. They are fairly thick, and are not slippy, with a kind of rough coating. They are white and opaque. Make sure you get the right set for your size of instrument (i.e. soprano, tenor etc.), and choose high or low G-string.

In my view, Aquilas are superb strings for beginner

instruments, and can bring even the cheapest uke to life. They are loud, have loads of 'bell like' sustain and are quite bright sounding. Some people, however, don't like them - they are thicker than some strings, and if you are an absolute beginner, they can hurt the fingers. The rough coating can also make a noise when you slide your fingers on them that some people don't like. For me though, as a guitar player - my fingers are used to the soreness, and the noise you get from wound strings. If they don't sound right for you, take a look at the next suggestion. That said, I would suggest you go through the pain barrier, if you are a beginner, that is going to happen anyway. I suggest it because if you have a ukulele that cost less than £100, I would wager that Aquila strings would be the best change you can make. They have a real knack of turning a cheap ukulele into something quite special. I put Aquilas on my Makala Dolphin ukuleles as a matter of course.

Worth

These are Japanese strings, and come in a bewildering range of styles. As well as size styles, they come in different thicknesses, and two colours (brown and clear). I personally like the Brown Mediums, labelled as BM (well... duh!). These strings are thinner than Aquilas, and are smooth in finish (so slippy). I think they also have less tension, and are easier on the fingers. They sing better than Aquila to my ears when picked, but I prefer Aquilas when strummed. Horses for courses I suppose. They work very well on mahogany instruments. Some say there is no difference between the brown and clear strings, but to my ears, the brown are mellower. Worths generally I find are a mellower sound than Aquila and work very well on more expensive instruments. If you bought your first uke at a price above £100, I would seriously consider giving them a go.

Others

Other strings I have tried and enjoy include Kala Red's, Ko'Aloau Golds and Martin strings. With regard to the latter, note that that Martin makes two types of string – nylon, and fluorocarbon. It is widely accepted that the fluorocarbon strings are much nicer sounding and hold their tuning much better. They have a real bell like chime on solid wood instruments and they are the string of choice on my Mainland ukulele.

Have fun - but I do urge you - if you have an entry-level instrument with cheap strings - upgrade - it is well, well worth the effort. Bear in mind though, the above is only a guide. Whilst I always recommend Aquila for cheaper instruments, if you have more expensive ukulele I would actually recommend you try a few different types of string until you find the brand that sounds right for your particular instrument.

10. HOW TO CHANGE UKULELE STRINGS

So I have just told you of the benefits of trying alternative types of ukulele string, you bought a pack, but now what? Trust me, it's not so hard to do.

Firstly though, this isn't a complete step-by-step guide to changing strings, more just a guide. The reason I cant do it totally step by step, is that the way you tie strings to bridge varies, and some people prefer there own methods. People also prefer their own way of tying to the tuning peg. My tip here - copy the tying done on the uke you bought!! (They are basic knots really)

So, my tips:

- Tie one end of the new string onto bridge as per the old string (do them one at a time to copy the old strings!). String 1 in your packet is the one nearest the floor, string 4, the one nearest your face. You will either have a tie bridge or a bridge with notches. If it is a tie bridge, the string goes through the hole and is then doubled around itself a couple of times and tied off at the base. For a notched bridge, you tie a substantial enough knot in the end of the string to hold it in place. For either method, when the string is on, give it a substantial pull (don't worry, the bridge is designed to hold a lot of tension). This is important, as you need to ensure that the knot will hold or you are wasting your time.

- Run the string to the peg end, pass through the peg, and round once, and through hole again. Some people prefer to tie them - that is good too, and you may find if your strings slip it's essential. The important thing is to avoid it slipping. Because the string is nylon, it will stretch with time, so when you have doubled it at the peg end, keep it taught down the length of the uke before you start winding or you will end up with far too much wrapped around the peg and cause yourself tuning problems. If when the string is taught you have the string wrapped so many times on the peg that it is overlapping itself you started winding with the string too loose.

- Then, tighten the peg to pitch getting the string to wind once around the top of the hole (over the string) and the rest winding down towards the headstock - I would invest in a couple of things here - a peg winder (very cheap) and a digital tuner (though you can tune to pitch with pipes, tuning forks, piano etc.). Digital tuners are cheap and they make things so easy and accurate. Purists will shout at me here for not encouraging tuning to ear.... yadda yadda - I am trying to encourage beginners, not give them another skill to learn...... Try not to have too many coils around the post as I say above. If you do, be brave and take the string off and wind it again.

- Repeat on all the other strings.

- You can then go back to your first string - pluck it and you will find it has gone flat. This is because the string is stretched and perfectly normal. You can either retune, play a little, then leave it and re-tune next time, but that will take a long time for the strings to settle. You can speed this process along a few ways - but my method - put your forefinger under string and pull away from the neck about half inch or so and hold it for a few seconds. Retune, repeat, retune repeat, retune repeat. Eventually you will find you need to retune less and less. But do be careful with this -don't overdo it - you may well snap the string. If you find that the string appears to be constantly stretching and is never in tune, you may have a string slipping at the peg or the bridge (check your knots / loops) or you may have a defective or loose tuning peg.

- Keep the spare string coiled at the

headstock - if your sting snaps at the bridge, you can re-use it. Some people snip them to look tidy. That's fine.

Good luck - it really is very easy. If you make a mistake, the nylon strings are easily re-usable, or cheap if you snap them all! However, bear this in mind – if you are enjoying playing the ukulele, you WILL be changing a lot of strings in your lifetime, so there really is not putting this job off. In my view, this is one of the first things you should learn – like changing a tire on a car.

11. ALL ABOUT WOOD

Something has been bothering me for quite a while. It's not an ingrowing toenail, it's something far more serious.. In fact, that 'something' has been bothering me all the time I have been buying guitars, let alone ukuleles, and that 'something' didn't change when I bought my first ukulele. In fact I just saw that the confusion (and the potential rip-off) continue.

If you are new to stringed instruments in this family (the chordophone family since you are asking.. top of the class for me!) and are looking to buy a ukulele, you may notice listings and adverts making reference to "solid" wood, "solid tops", "all solid" and the like. When you read this, are you absolutely sure what is being sold here? - Worse still is there some misrepresentation going on? (Don't worry, I am naming no names, and my lawyers are on standby..)

The basics of wooden ukuleles (as with wooden

acoustic guitars) is this - the wood that makes the instrument is either an actual thin slice of solid wood, or it is a laminate of lots and lots of thin pieces of wood with a nice looking veneer on the outer visible edge. This applies to the wood on the soundboard or top (the piece with the hole in it!) , the sides of the body, and the back. The wood is one or the other. It's solid (totally solid) or it isn't. There is no in-between.

The general difference in most wooden instruments is that a solid piece of wood is generally the best tonally, and laminate is worst. I say general, as this is also dependent on the type of wood and type of instrument, but for the purposes of a general buyers guide, it is generally accepted that top quality is "all solid top, back and sides", medium is "solid top" and the cheaper end is "laminate all over".

The other thing that comes in to play is, of course, price, as all solid instruments cost a good deal more than laminates - and I fully appreciate that we all have to cut our cloth accordingly. This isn't a chapter about sneering (and believe me, there are a lot of players out there who sneer), I fully understand that for some, a laminate may be the only option (I own some!!)

But what REALLY concerns me is where ukuleles are advertised, (and I have to say, eBay is mainly the place where you will find this), where the description of the woods is less than clear.

I recently saw a baritone ukulele for sale on eBay at what was clearly an inflated price compared to what it could be bought for in a store. Worse still, the seller had it listed as a solid mahogany wood ukulele, despite it clearly being a laminate top and body model. I was so annoyed that I emailed the buyer to point out that his listing was incorrect, and he replied saying it was a laminate of sheets of mahogany, and therefore it was ALL mahogany, and therefore SOLID mahogany...... !!!!? The item sold to some unlucky buyer, - a total rip-off. New buyers take note!

The manufacturer websites don't help either - and

nothing annoys me more than those that don't say whether the instruments are solid or not. Many do it, and I really don't understand why. Well, actually, I do. They do it because they try to capitalise on the confusion.

I stress again, buying an instrument that isn't totally solid is NOT a bad thing, but you should be clear what you are buying, whatever you buy - surely?

Therefore, please, do take care - if you see a 'bargain' uke at anything under £100 - £150 claiming to be all solid wood I would exercise some serious caution (not rule it out totally, just be cautious). Email the buyer. Ask the question directly, "is the ukulele a totally solid ukulele, is the wood in the ukulele cut from one single piece of wood, or is it thin strips glued together"?

If your ukulele arrives and it is not what it says it is, complain. If the seller cannot be clear with you, avoid the seller and / or the ukulele. You need to get what you pay for.

I am often asked how to tell if the instrument is solid wood if you get to actually hold it - it isn't totally straightforward, but some tips:

- On a solid top instrument, you should be able to look at the edge of the inside of the sound hole and see whether the grains on outer edge run "through" the wood. Imagine looking end on at a thick piece of wood such as a skirting board - the grain would run through - it is no different on a ukulele top - just thinner! Look at the edge of the sound hole and see if you can follow the grain on the top running down in stripes on the edge of the hole. On a cheap laminate ukulele, you should be able to see the laminated layers of wood. Things get tricky if the top or inside of sound hole is painted. This is sometimes a case of the maker trying to hide the laminate (and dare I say it, dress up a pigs ear as something else), but not always! Bruko put a binding on the inside of some of their sound holes by way of decoration but Bruko make totally solid wonderful instruments.

- For the back and sides - if you can see the outer grain through varnish - look inside the instrument with a torch - do the grains on the inside match the patterns on the outside - if they do you have a pretty good sign it is solid back or sides. The very cheapest laminated backs and sides have grains going in opposite directions which is a dead give-away!

So be aware, as with most things in life, things are not always what they seem. I do get annoyed at limited information for new buyers - always remember, buyer beware, and if a deal seems too good to be true, it "probably" is...

12. MORE ABOUT WOOD

Beyond brand names and sizes, probably the most talked about topic when it comes to ukulele is the wood they are made of. In fact, when you are on the path to buying your first uke, you will probably find your mind boggled at the choices.

The differences in wood discussions (and tonally, we are referring to the wood the body is made of) will tend to be either whether it's solid or laminate or what type of wood it is. In this chapter we discuss that issue in a little more detail.

Solid versus Laminate

This refers to the thin pieces of wood that make up the top, back and sides of the body of the ukulele. In simple terms, solid wood is just that, a thin slice of wood taken in one piece from the tree, and laminate refers to thin veneers of wood glued together in a sandwich, rather like plywood.

Solid wood will unarguably give you the better sweeter sound, and in many cases better volume. Without getting too technical, it's simply that the solid piece of wood can naturally resonate and sing better than laminated wood. Laminated wood has layers of glue or resin that also need to vibrate, and this can affect the tone of the instrument.

Solid wood instruments are also much more expensive, so you will find the vast majority of cheaper (under £100) instruments will be either all or part laminate (you can get instruments with solid tops but laminate back and sides which is a kind of 'halfway house'). The cheapest all solid wood instruments that I would recommend are those made by Brüko.

So, is solid better? Well I'd have to say yes, and the expensive top end instruments are ALL solid. That said, if you are a beginner, there are some great laminate instruments like those in the Lanikai range and the Makalas. Additionally (to confuse further) the superb instruments made by Fluke are actually laminate wood tops, but they get their signature sound from the design and plastic backs (more on that later). The point to remember is it really is the quality of the overall instrument that counts. A badly made instrument made of solid wood, may well sound terrible compared to a decent, well made laminate ukulele, made from quality laminated wood. Have I confused things enough?

Types of wood

Beyond the solid versus laminate debate, you will also want to consider the type of wood you are buying. To be perfectly honest I think this is very subjective. Wood type DOES change sound, but for better or worse depends totally on your ears - you need to try them out! Let's just say that the wood type alters the sound.

With laminates, you really don't want to worry about wood type – it's just a laminate, and anyone who tells you it is a 'special' laminate is trying to hoodwink you.

If you are going solid though, the most common wood you will currently come across for the ukulele is mahogany. As well as looking great (it really shines and sparkles under a good finish), it gives a lovely warm tone to the sound. Other wood types you will find include spruce (a brighter bouncy tone) cedar (again warmer) and the traditional wood for ukuleles, koa. (Be aware, solid koa instruments are hugely expensive!). You may also find woods like mango, acacia, ash, walnut and zebrawood.

This player can't tell you what sounds good, or what looks nice to you (these different woods all look totally different!) so have a play yourself. If the ukulele sounds good, you are most of the way there with what is important, but I fully understand that looks of an instrument are hugely important. What I never agree with though is looks over substance. As such, I would never buy a "cheap" koa ukulele unless I had played it, and I always suspicious of ukuleles with exotic looking woods being sold for prices that seem to bely their so called exotic nature.

If you are beginning and finding it difficult to decide, I think you really can't go wrong with mahogany though. Mahogany sounds good, looks good and is not too expensive.

Other Thoughts

Other than the above, which is mainly concerned with tone, you will find other woods for necks and fingerboards but these genuinely are just cosmetic factors. The wood used in a neck or a fingerboard will have no bearing on the way the ukulele sounds. Many players (rightly) like a smooth feel on the neck, so the finish on the wood is probably more important that the wood itself. Fingerboards can be made from a range of materials from the ultra cheap plywood stained black, to the more common rosewood or ebony. I prefer a nice real wood fingerboard with a dark colour (such as rosewood or ebony) but that is just me. The fingerboard is usually a thin piece of dark wood glued on to the flat face of the neck, but many old ukuleles, and some modern ukuleles have the frets applied directly into the neck wood itself. As I say, this is just cosmetic.

Further confusion comes when we consider the many plastic backed bodies like Flea, Fluke, Applause and Dolphins. You can also buy carbon fibre bodies, cigar box bodies and ukuleles made out of biscuit tins, but I suppose they are for another chapter!

Shop around, try to play, feel and listen to the ukulele and don't be drawn in by fancy looks over quality.

13. ALL ABOUT TUNING PEGS

Important things pegs, tuning pegs that is. They hold what is probably the most important end of the string. They have big job to do those pegs. Lets spare a moment and think about them.

If you are starting out with ukuleles you may get confused by the two most common types of tuners and which is best. This chapter serves to explain what you are most likely to see.

The two types of tuner you are likely to see are friction tuners, and geared tuners. Friction tuners, as their name suggests are tightened by a screw into the headstock of the ukulele, and the friction of their contact into the housing keeps them held fast. Geared tuners are like those you would see on a guitar, and the peg is connected to a gear which turns another gear connected to the tuning post. In the case of geared tuners, the physics of the gear mechanism keeps them held firm. As you can imagine, a tuning peg that doesn't hold the string firm, is not much use at all.

Friction tuners certainly look the part and have an old fashioned look that I think suits the ukulele. In the 1950's when the ukulele had it's first big boom, you would have seen very little else on the instrument. They do take getting used to though as the lack of gearing means the turns you apply to the tuner move the posts directly and as such you don't have a great amount of sensitive control. (Unless we are talking planetary tuners, but more on that later, let's not complicate things....)

Geared tuners are 'generally' trouble free but unless nicely styled can look out of place on a small ukulele. A pet hate of mine on cheaper ukuleles are geared tuners that are clearly too heavy for the instrument. A heavy tuning peg will make the head of the ukulele heavy and tend to drop when you are holding it. (Beware cheap ukuleles that use guitar tuners - too big, too heavy, and make the uke look like Mickey Mouse!)

You will read in forums that some people can't

abide one or the other, and the opinions are definitely split. I have a different view. I think both types are great so long as you consider the cost and the ukulele they are fitted to. In my experience, very cheap ukuleles with friction pegs tend to have pegs that are nothing but trouble. A cheap friction tuner that just won't bite is useless. Geared tuners on a cheap ukulele work very well, and in most cases can be trouble free, but beware; there are bad geared tuners too! If you can see the instrument, check the tuners out. Do they *look* cheap? Is there unnecessary movement or 'play' when you tweak them? If so, reject the instrument.

If you buy a good beginner instrument, like a Makala, or Lanikai, you should be OK whatever they are. But do try both! My collection has some of each!

If you are having trouble with your tuners, a slight tweak and service can sometimes work wonders. For both geared and friction tuners, the common slipping problem encountered with both can often be solved with a 'careful' tightening of the screw that holds the peg to the head of the ukulele (don't overdo it!). Geared tuners can also get sticky, making tuning a little staggered or stuttered. Application of a tiny amount of all in one bike oil to the gears can solve these problems. If, however, there is play on either type of tuner when tightened, the chances are, the tuner is defective and you will forever have problems with tuning. Thankfully, even if you have a ukulele you cannot return, tuners are easily replaced, and there are a multitude of stores offering replacements.

And finally, a word about planetary tuners. These are essentially friction tuners, but with an internal gearing mechanism in the housing. They look like 'fat' friction tuners, but the clever stuff hidden inside gives the benefits of geared tuning in a peg that has a traditional look. The best of both worlds. They are however expensive, and you are unlikely to see them on a beginner ukulele.

14. CLEANING AND MAINTAINING YOUR UKULELE

This is a question that is often asked on ukulele forums, and I thought it would be helpful to give you my perspective on cleaning, treating and maintaining the ukulele.

CLEANING

I will start off by stating that a ukulele, if looked after, really shouldn't need a great deal of cleaning. If it does, then what the heck are you doing with it??! That said, if you are gigging, camping etc., you may find that the instrument becomes dirty with grime, sweat, beer (!), and just day to day playing will cause a build up of grease and oil from your hands. Mix this with natural dust and you get a claggy ukulele!

I will also add from the start that the instrument cleaning business is a lucrative market but in my view 95% of the products on offer are overkill. They can be avoided completely in my view if you keep a lint free soft cloth in your ukulele case and EVERY time you finish playing you give the whole instrument a polish all over. Do this regularly and I think you will rarely need any sort of cleaning fluid or polish.

If you ARE interested in cleaning and sprucing up your ukulele read on.

Bodies

Cleaning the body of the ukulele will depend on how dirty the instrument has become. If you have dried on grime on there, mud, beer, whatever - the best thing to do is to clean off with a barely damp lint free cloth to remove the solids, then polish with a dry clean cloth.

If you have a gloss or painted body uke, you can give a bit of showroom shine using a small (tiny) amount of guitar polish on a soft cloth and polishing according to the instructions. Be careful though - make sure your cloth is super, super soft with no debris on it. The sign of an over polished instrument are swirl marks in the varnish, rather like on an over polished car. Treat your ukulele as you would cleaning your Ferrari! (What do you mean you don't have one??)

If you are using a polish - keep it well away from the fingerboard and strings! Guitar polish is a synthetic product designed to be applied to gloss coatings or metal areas. You do not want such a product getting into the open grain of a fingerboard, into the nut slots, or building up around the frets. Ensure all polish is removed from the instrument when polishing to stop build up of polish.

If you have a natural finish ukulele in matte - be very careful. In my youth I learned a lesson with such an instrument by applying polish, which then sunk into the grain and left my instrument covered in white specks that were impossible to remove. Not a good look!

Hardware

If you have pearly, plastic or chrome tuning pegs and strap buttons, they really should only need a buff with a soft cloth. That said, a wipe with the cloth with which you applied polish should not be a problem so long as you ensure that you have removed all deposits of polish from around the tuners or in the hard to reach gaps.

Fingerboard

The fingerboard, if natural wood and not painted is a different animal. Do not apply polish to it as you may cause it to expand and then have problems with frets rising or falling out. You also stand the risk of the polish becoming embedded in the grain of the fingerboard leaving white specks. If you have a ukulele with a seriously grimy fingerboard in-between the frets, you can VERY carefully and lightly rub between them with a super fine grain wire wool to remove the gunk and get back to the wood. This should be enough to remove deposits on even the dirtiest fingerboard, but remember - a routine of wiping the instrument down with soft cloth after each session, particularly UNDER the strings should remove the need for you to ever do this.

You can also think about treating your fingerboard with a bore oil to feed the wood and prevent it becoming too dry and cracking (avoid lemon oil sold in guitar shops - it is synthetic) I use Fret Doctor bore oil, which is the choice of oil for woodwind instrument players. It is a totally natural product that feeds the wood. The bore oil needs to be applied very lightly (just a smear), left to dry and then polished off. One of the worst things you can do with a fingerboard is over treat it as this can permanently damage your instrument. The regularity in applying oil depends on your climate but certainly not more than twice a year is needed. If your neck looks obviously dry you can consider a treatment.

Strings

Being made of nylon, strings on the ukulele don't deteriorate as quickly as steel strings on a guitar. That said, it is nice to keep them clean as they do pick up oils from your fingers over time. Simply ensure you wipe your strings down after each session - a good habit to form that will also clean your neck and fingerboard in the process.

And as a final word on cleaning the ukulele, the best advice is to keep your uke in a quality case when you are not playing to keep the dust off!

HUMIDITY

Humidity in the atmosphere can have the effect of causing serious damage to a ukulele. It should be born in mind that this issue mainly affects solid wood instruments. Wood is a natural material and it changes by expanding and contracting as it takes on or loses moisture from the air around it.

Lose moisture and there is a risk of the fingerboard shrinking, the instrument cracking or distorting if left unchecked for too long a period of time. Too much humidity and you can find the top of the instrument swelling and similar distortions. At best this can cause cosmetic issues with the ukulele, but at worst can throw the instrument permanently out.

Before you start to panic though, the requirement to keep a check on humidity only applies to those of you with instruments in locations with humidity at either extreme (those in the far east, or Arizona, take note)

The best humidity for a wooden instrument is between 45% and 55%. If you have a humidity gauge and are regularly falling way below or above this level you should think about your options.

In a dry climate, you may want to consider investing in a humidifier – this is a small device that lives in the ukulele case, or hangs inside the sound hole that contains a sponge material that holds water. The water is then given off through evaporation and keeps the instrument in a more humid atmosphere. Ensure you purchase a product designed for the ukulele, as you need to ensure it maintains that ideal humidity level.

If you live in a very humid country, then your problem is tougher to solve and you may need to consider a de-humidifier for the room your ukulele is kept in.

In addition to the above, do not keep your instrument in an overly hot or cold room, next to a heater or radiator, or in direct sunlight!

15. ALL ABOUT NUTS AND SADDLES

We have looked at strings, woods and tuners, so it is about time I moved on to some guidance on the other important parts of a ukulele.

The ukulele works by holding the strings in tension over a sound chamber to resonate the sound - as a child you may have done the same thing with rubber bands and a tissue box. In order to make this play accurately, some maths is required. For the frets to accurately and uniformly change the notes of the strings when held, it is important that the string length is accurately fixed and set in relation to those frets. The parts of the ukulele that hold the strings at the correct length are the nut (at the top end of the uke by the tuners) and the saddle, held in the piece of wood glued on to the body of the uke below the sound hole. The saddle actually usually sits in a wooden mount called the bridge, but commonly the whole assembly is called the bridge. The distance between these two is the scale length and the position of the frets is linked directly to this scale length. If the scale length is too short or too long for the position of the frets, the instrument will never be capable of being accurately tuned.

As with all stringed instruments, the quality of these parts and how they are shaped is critical to an accurate playing experience. As well as the scale length being critical, too much height at the saddle and you will have too high an 'action', too low and you will get buzzing as the strings touch the frets. Action is the term used to describe how high off the fingerboard the strings run. Quite simply, a high action is both difficult to play and can throw the tuning out.

Likewise at the nut - if the slots are cut too low, you will get buzzing at the low frets, too high and you raise action, and worse can cause a sharpening of notes when pressed at the 1st and 2nd frets.

In both cases, if the string is not as parallel to the fingerboard as is possible without buzzing you can get into 'intonation' problems. I will deal with intonation in more detail later in this book, but it bad intonation generally just means that the correct notes don't play at the respective frets.

Adjusting action for accurate tuning and to remove buzzes is something I will cover in a subsequent chapter also, but on a nicely set up instrument if you hold a string at both the 1st and (say) 12th fret, you should be able to just slip a thin business card between the string and fret at or around the 6th.

So what are these items made of? Well in cheaper instruments, almost certainly plastic, or a composite material, which is basically plastic, but is trying to 'big itself up' by calling it something else (stand up please NuBone and Tusq). In more expensive instruments, these parts may well be made of bone, or a hardwood like Ebony. That is certainly preferable. If you think about it, the nut and the saddle are the two key parts that the string touches. These are the elements that hold that string in perfect position and tension and allow it to sing. A good quality material can only improve the quality of the vibration, and the clarity of the tone. Bone is considered to be the best material to help with this.

Some players may also find their ukulele saddle isn't a strip held in a wooden mount, but rather the saddle is a single piece. Flea ukuleles are like this, as are some top end ukes. They are called on piece saddles, but you will note that they do the same thing. The only difference is that they are not removable and difficult to adjust and as such, their accurate placing and shaping when the instrument was manufactured is absolutely critical.

As a final thought - if you are fiddling with your saddle and remove it to take it down in height and lower your action, remember - this is the key point of the instrument that transfers sound into the body of the uke. It is essential the base of the saddle is sanded totally flat and when re-seated makes a perfect fit into the bridge mount. This is even more important if you have a piezo pick up fitted under the saddle, as you may find a badly seated saddle results in volume differences across strings (not good).

16. INTONATION

Into what now?

You may hear this term used a many times in relation to all sorts of stringed instruments, and simply it relates to the accuracy of the instrument. The important thing to note is you want GOOD intonation, or perfect intonation. Bad or poor intonation is a bad bad thing, and in extreme cases may mean the ukulele you have is always going to be unplayable unless you take drastic re-building action.

Intonation refers to the accuracy of the frets in providing the right notes when fretted. The frets are laid out mathematically in relation to the scale length of the instrument to allow for this, but the accuracy depends on their spacing and the distance between the bridge and the nut. The mathematics also assumes that your strings are as close to parallel to the fingerboard as possible. Your strings on your standard uke are tuned GCEA when open, but when you fret at certain point; each fretted note should be an accurate note in itself (or its perfect sharp version). If you look on the Got A Ukulele website, you can download a fretboard roadmap showing the notes that should be played on each fret space of the instrument. You can check your notes with a tuner at any position. If your intonation is off, the instrument may well play in tune on the open strings, but as soon as you start using the frets (which is a rather critical part of the playing process!), you will find that the instrument sounds out of tune. Some people try to correct this by ignoring the tuner, adjusting the strings so the chord they have played is in tune. This is bad practice, if you do this; you are just compounding the problem, and will probably find your open strings are now out of tune.

The way to quickly check intonation on a ukulele is to tune it, and then fret the string at the 12th fret and play it. The note you hear should be exactly one octave higher than the open string. If it is sharp or flat from the open note, the intonation is off.

What can I do about it?

Well, if the difference is slight, it may simply be down to the action being too high. I have owned ukuleles where intonation was bad 'out of the box', and I dropped the bridge saddle a millimetre and it sorted it. This was a simple case of the strings not running as parallel to the fingerboard as necessary. It may also be a case of action being too high at the nut - be very careful here lower the nut slots too much and it is very hard to go back – as you want there to be about a credit cards thickness between the string and the top of the first fret. It could also be a bad string - try changing it. If those more simple changes don't fix your problem, then I am afraid it is most probably more serious (i.e. the bridge is not set in the right place or the frets are poorly spaced) and I would avoid the instrument! Some cheap ukes are just built plain wrong!

Some poorly made instruments may also have frets that are too high, and fretting firmly can stretch the strings into the gaps giving off notes - this is not a case of bad intonation, but it is still a bad set up and I would reject it.

Anyway - no matter what you are spending - if the intonation is off and it is down to the way the thing is built, it will never play right - avoid it!

I provide below my checklist on how to try to deal with intonation.

1. Bad strings? A badly made string can cause tuning problems along its length - try swapping the string to see if that cures it.

2. Action at the saddle? This refers to the height of the saddle. If a saddle is too low, it can cause buzzing but equally, if too high, can cause problems with intonation. Again, this comes down to mathematics (switch your brain on and think of Pythagoras!). For the maths to work, and the frets to accurately give you the right notes, it assumes that the strings run as close as possible as to be parallel with the line of the fingerboard. If you imagine a seriously high saddle, the strings will run at an increasing height away from the fingerboard

approaching the bridge - like the hypotenuse of a long thin triangle - if this is the case, your open tuned string will sound fine, but you are stretching and pushing the string down when fretting and this will give you an off note. The answer is simple - sand the saddle base down and re-install, taking care not to sand too much or you will get buzzing, do it a little, replace it, repeat.

3. Action at the nut? This is trickier to deal with, and may be something you give to a luthier or trusted guitar technician. Again if the nut slots are too high, you get same effect in reverse. To lower the nut slots be very very careful and I would recommend using nut files especially for the purpose. These are specialist tools that come in a range of thicknesses designed exactly for this job. Some people claim success using the edge of a nail file, or a length of wound guitar string, but I would be very careful with those not to widen the nut slot, as that is not the aim of the exercise. Go very slowly, this is a difficult adjustment to reverse!

4. High frets? In some cases high frets can cause

problems, as the string will have to dip down as you press it and stretch - characteristics of this are a note that sounds fine when held softly but sharpens when you squeeze. The dramatic cure is to have the frets dressed down, but a much easier fix is to play the uke a little lighter with your fretting hand!

5. Something more serious? Sadly, if the above don't fix the issue, you are looking at a badly made uke or a neck out of alignment. Either get a refund, or it is a valuable oldie consider paying for a fix.

17. SHOULD I PLAY WITH A PICK?

This is another extremely common question - do you play the ukulele with a plectrum or pick (the small plastic things you see guitarists using to pick the strings)?

Personally speaking, I don't - I really don't see the need, and find that if I do play with a pick; the sound can be a bit overpowering and sharp. Tradition suggests that the ukulele should be strummed with the fingers and thumb - held cuddled against the body in a variety of fingerstyles, but generally using the first finger, with some thumb for accenting or other fingers in a fan style.

If you have short nails you WILL get a softer sound, which is often the reason people resort to a pick, but growing the first finger nail will add to your "attack", and isn't really that hard to do.

All of that said, a trawl of YouTube would show you

that plenty of people do play with a pick, so it isn't "wrong". So long as you are making a nice noise with your ukulele, you can pick it with whatever you like! (Within reason..)

What I would however suggest, is to go for a specific ukulele felt or leather pick which will help avoid damage to the finish of your uke, and to the strings themselves. Nylon strings will not stand up to very much abuse from a heavy handed pick, and very few ukuleles I have seen have a scratch guard fitted as you would see on a guitar to protect the finish. If you really do want to play with a guitar pick, I would urge you to pick more softly and be more precise with how you use it.

A final choice worth mentioning is the use of finger picks that you may see banjo players use. These would be good for fingerstyle playing if you cannot grow your fingernails, but again, take care with them, and don't whatever you do, use the metal ones!

18. DEALING WITH BUZZES AND RATTLES

This is probably the biggest issue many will have with the ukulele. What is that annoying buzz when I play? In the best case it will be something simple like technique, but in the worst case can signal something serious like a flawed uke. This is, naturally, more common with cheaper ukuleles but sadly can affect even the most expensive uke if it is not set up correctly.

Discussion forums are awash with theories and advice (some useful, some not so) on how to deal with such problems, so I thought it useful to give my own thoughts. I have structured these from the simple to the serious, so if you have a buzz you can work your way through the list and hopefully solve your problem at an early stage before things get difficult. Don't be tempted to jump ahead as these tips are structured, hopefully saving you time, money and tears.

Is it your technique?

Getting a clean sound from a ukulele depends on good technique with your fretting fingers. Ensure you are pressing the strings perpendicular to the neck and squarely between the frets. Ensure your fingers are not touching other strings. This will be difficult at first but practice, as it will take time for your fingers to become accustomed to the strange positions your ukulele brain is telling them to adopt. Sometimes buzzes can also occur due to over strumming or the position of the strum. Calm it down a little, strum at the end of the fingerboard in that sweet spot we talked about.

Is it actually the strings causing the problem?

Buzzes don't always come from the strings themselves, so check the rest of the ukulele. Are the tuner fittings tight? Are there any other fittings that are coming loose (such as strap buttons or pickup switches)? Another often overlooked culprit is string coils at the headstock, or the bits left over where you tie them on the bridge - trim them if they are causing the buzz. If there is anything more structurally unsound with the ukulele that is buzzing, like the back is hanging off, or any binding is loose I would think about having the instrument exchanged if it is new. If it is used, see if it can be repaired.

Is it a case of bad strings?

Due to the nature of ukulele strings, it is possible to get a bad string in a pack and this needs to be ruled out in locating your buzz. Can you isolate the particular string that is buzzing? It may be worth swapping it, or another odd tip that often works, take it off and string it the other way around. This can solve problems where manufacturing has left a thin or thick spot on the string. (Some people have laughed at me when I have suggested that, but then looked rather sheepish when they found it worked!)

Action at the saddle?

We are now getting into more difficult territory, but still relatively easily fixed. If the saddle at the bridge is too low the strings are likely to vibrate against frets when strummed. Take off or loosen the strings and pull out the saddle carefully with long nosed pliers (it's the white thin strip of plastic or bone). To raise it you have two options. Either put a thin shim (or two) of wood veneer in the base of the saddle slot, replace saddle and strum. The veneer strips need to be very very thin, a fraction of a millimetre. Some people have used card or paper, but I would prefer to use wood to keep the bond between the saddle and the ukulele as good as possible. The alternative is to purchase a new saddle, and cut and shape it very slightly higher than old one. These are cheap to buy and with careful use of a piece of sandpaper is not really a difficult job to re-create the same shape. Your aim here is to raise it just enough to stop the buzzing, and for that we are talking fractions of a millimetre. Raise it too much and you will cause intonation issues and create a high action that is difficult to play.

A note here also about fixed saddles. Some ukuleles (Fleas, Flukes, some high end models) have a one piece moulded and shaped bridge and saddle. It is NOT possible to raise these saddles without serious luthier work. If you have a buzz, and have made it this far, have a look through the rest of the guide, and if you are still buzzing, you seriously need to have it replaced.

Action at the nut?

We are in genuinely difficult territory. If the slots in the nut that the strings are on are too deep you are likely to get buzzes particularly on the lower frets. The fix for this is more difficult and you may now want to seriously consider going to a luthier or guitar technician. To try yourself you either need to fit a new nut (carefully tap out old nut and replace, filing down the slots to suit action without buzzing) or try something cleverer!

I have successfully raised nut slots individually by

taking a spare saddle and sanding it making sure to collect the dust that is created. Apply a drop of super glue to the dust and quickly mix with a cocktail stick then fill in the offending nut slot (very carefully). Breathe on it to start curing the glue and leave it overnight. What you have done is create a hard invisible fill in the nut slot. When totally dry and hardened, you can then file into this filled gap to create a new slot at a height that doesn't buzz.

Others

If you have worked through the above steps in order and still have a buzzing ukulele, then I am afraid you may have serious problems. You may have an offending fret that is too high and needs to be filed down. I would recommend a luthier or guitar tech doing this for you, as making a mistake here will potentially require new frets. Persistent buzzes may also signify a badly made uke, a neck out of alignment, or a bowed neck. If this is the case, and the instrument is new I would return it. If it's an old or used instrument the decision whether to get it professionally fixed will depend entirely on the value of the instrument. I would consider getting a vintage Martin fixed, but not a Makala Dolphin!

I hope this is of use and helps remove any panic you may have. Buzzes are common and in the vast majority of cases are simple to solve. Just work down the list and good luck!

19. HOW TO READ UKULELE TABLATURE (TABS)

If you have bought yourself a ukulele, you are presumably using the vast resources of the Internet to download some songs and chords.

Sheets with lyrics with the chord name typed above are easy to follow; you just strum the chord shown at the appropriate point in the song. The alternative is the tablature format (or tabs) which show a representation of the neck of the uke, and use numbers on the strings to show which fret to hold when that string is plucked or strummed. These can be used for showing chords, but are somewhat overkill for that, and are more commonly used to show fingerpicking styles, or perhaps a run of a melody within a strummed song that needs to be picked out.

The tablature is laid in with four horizontal parallel lines on the page, representing the ukulele strings with the G at the bottom and the A at the top. A number shown on one of those strings means to hold the string at that fret and pluck it. All very simple. In reading tabs, you will, however, find a range of other strange symbols that mean nothing to you. This guide talks you through the most common ones you will see.

h=Hammer on

This is the action of "hammering down" or in plain English, putting the finger on a string that has already been plucked at another fret without picking it again. This changes the already vibrating string sound to the new-fretted note and is a nice effect you will hear in all sorts of music. You may see it written on tabs like the example below, which means to pluck the string at the 7th fret, and whilst it is still ringing to place a finger on the same string but at the 9th.

```
e|-------7h9-----------
```

p=Pull off

This is the opposite of the hammer on, where you release the string that has been hammered on. You may see it like the example below, which follows the example above - and it means to pluck the string at the seventh, hammer on to the 9th, and then release the finger from the 9th whilst still ringing, allowing the string to go back to the 7th. To execute a clean sounding pull off, you may need to try to drag and pluck the string a little as your finger leaves it.

e|-------7h9p7-----------

\ or / or s = Slides

This is the action of plucking the string at a certain fret, and then whilst it is still ringing, sliding the fretting finger either up or down the string to another fret whilst it is still ringing. / usually means to slide up, and \ to slide down. 's' means both. In the following example it means to pluck the string at the 5th, and whilst it is ringing slide up to the 9th.

```
e|------5/9-------------
```

b or ^ = Bends.

This is the action of bending the string whilst holding it at a fret to change the pitch to another note. This is usually shown on tabs by following the bend symbol with the note you are bending up to. For example

```
e|--------5b7----------
```

means to pluck the string at the 5th, and and with the finger held on the 5th, bend the string to the pitch of the 7th fret. You do this by pulling the string across the neck to physically bend or stretch it.

v or ~ = Vibrato

Vibrato is that shimmery wobbly effect you get by effectively shaking the string. It is usually achieved by holding the fretted string and rocking the finger up and down or side to side. It is tricky to master but gives a great effect.

An example would be

```
e|-------13vvvvvvv---------
```

and the number of symbols is indicative of how long you should perform the vibrato.

20. SORE FINGERS?

Probably the biggest barrier to new ukulele players who have never played a stringed instrument before - sore fingers!

First, the bad news. There is very little I can suggest for the pain. I'm afraid it's something you just have to go through, and it is horrible. You will most likely get callouses or blisters and bruises on the tips of your fretting hand fingers from the pressing on the ukulele strings, and you may also get cramps or aches in your hand from making chord shapes. Both of these are perfectly natural - you are making your fingers make and hold positions they are not used to, you muscles and tendons need to learn and strengthen and your fingertips need to harden up from the abuse you are causing them.

I do have your sympathy, and would urge you to stick at it. It does get easier, and it would be such a shame for a beginner to give up ukulele because of sore fingers alone. (sadly, many do)

That said, I can provide you with some tips.

Practice!

Obvious really, keep at it to toughen up those fingertips and strengthen your hand. If the pain is bad, try to practice for shorter periods but more often. Practicing the ukulele only once a week will make it a long hard slog! You need to find the right balance, but without making yourself miserable with sore fingers.

Find other strengthening exercises

Some people swear by those grippy gadgets that mountain climbers use to strengthen their fingers, but those squeezy stress balls work just as well. Practice your gripping by squeezing these whenever you are not playing your uke. A friend swears by kneading bread dough as a good exercise!

Stretches

As well as building strength, you need your fretting hand to be flexible. When ever you are 'not playing your ukulele, try to introduce finger stretches into your day as often as possible. Stretch your fingers back and forth, make fists then spread your hands wide. Give those hands a workout!

Leave the blisters alone!

You may well get blisters appearing on your fingertips which are both unsightly and sore. Don't burst them or pick them! Players of any stringed instrument build up callouses of harder skin on their fingertips that prevent this happening very often and if you burst or pick at the blister you are only slowing down the hardening process. Resist the urge! A tip I heard on this subject is to dip your fingertips in surgical spirit a couple of times a day for 10 minutes or so, as this spirit hardens skin.

Also, don't be tempted to apply plasters / band-aids and then play, they will affect your learning and accuracy in placing chord shapes.

It is really just about breaking through the barrier, and when you do, you will forget the pain and hardly feel the strings as you play.

21. UKULELE PICKUPS

Whilst a ukulele is, in the main an acoustic instrument designed to play anywhere, you will find times when you want a little more power to your sound - when playing in a band alongside other instruments for example, or on stage. There is nothing wrong with wanting to amplify your little uke, and in fact it can be quite good fun!

You will therefore find that many ukuleles come with 'pickups' fitted - but what should you look out for?

Firstly, a pickup is just a term used for a device that either amplifies sound or vibrations in an instrument and turns it into a signal that can be played by an amplifier. Unlike an electric guitar, ukuleles use nylon strings, and therefore need a different sort of pickup than a magnetic coil type you see on electrics - those sort of pickups read the vibration of metal strings only using electromagnetism to do the work.

For a ukulele, you are going to come across two main types of pickup - microphonic or piezoelectric (piezo for short)

MICROPHONIC PICKUPS

As the name suggests a microphonic pickup is quite literally a small microphone fitted inside the ukulele connected to a jackpin (the bit the cable plugs in to). They are usually fitted on the end of a bendy bit of wire allowing you to position them inside the uke body to find the nicest sound spot. These sort of microphone pickups work, but they can give terrible feedback - I would personally avoid one unless you are spending a lot of money on a quality microphone, as the market is also flooded with cheap microphones.

PIEZO PICKUPS

Piezo pickups are by far the most common and are made out of a sheet or strip of piezoelectric crystals, sandwiched between thin sheets of metal, that act as a transducer. Vibrations on the body of the ukulele are "picked up" by the piezo crystals and they turn this into an electrical signal that can be turned into sound by an amplifier. Like all pickups, including microphonic pickups, they are connected to a jack pin for plugging a cable into and then connecting to an amplifier.

Piezo pickups come in two main flavours:

- Soundboard transducers- these are a flat round plate of piezo crystals sandwiched between two very thin metal sheets around the size of a pound coin (or a nickel). A cable runs from the pickup to the jack pin, and the pickup is quite literally stuck to the underside of the soundboard, usually near the bridge where it picks up vibrations from the top of the ukulele. These pickups work well, but can also suffer from a little feedback. They are the only choice for ukuleles with fixed bridge saddles like Flukes and Fleas as the alternative we deal with below relies on being able to sit under the saddle. If you are retro fitting a soundboard transducer, you can experiment with placement to find the nicest tone. More expensive models may come with two pickup disks to allow for a broader sound. You can also fit these pickups on the outside of the uke, with the cable external cable that is held in place with a velcro pad stuck to the body. This avoids drilling into your uke, but I think they look messy and I would be more concerned about the sticky pad damaging my external finish.

• Under saddle transducers - these are thin strip of piezo crystals in a very thin metal strip that is fed up through a small hole in the top of the ukulele bridge and lay flat directly underneath the saddle. They work in the same way as the soundboard transducers, but lie directly under the strings and can be better at controlling feedback. These are very common types of pickup though placing them flat and accurately is absolutely essential as a bad fitting can lead to differences in volume across the strings.

OTHER THINGS TO CONSIDER

• Active or Passive? - You will find that most pickups will come either active or passive. A passive pickup is connected directly to the jackpin and the amplifier does all the work increasing the sound. A small internal amplifier in the instrument, usually powered by a 9v battery, boosts an active pickup that gives the signal a lift and balance. Some say this provides for a better sound, but to be honest, I think all that depends on how good your amplifier is! Passive pickups will certainly need the amplifier input volume to be set a little higher. Active pickups also come with inconvenience of having a hole cut in your uke for the battery to fit into. They also stop working completely when the battery is flat.

- EQ's - Higher end pickup systems will provide a set of EQ controls (volume, bass, treble) on the side of your ukulele allowing you to "shape" the sound as it leaves the ukulele. This is a nice feature to have, though not essential if you don't mind tweaking your amplifier instead. The nicest feature in my opinion is the ability to adjust the volume, and between songs, kill the sound completely if you want to. The downside is yet another hole cut in the side of your uke for the control panel. I personally find these overkill on an instrument like a ukulele

- Brands? - As with most things in life - you gets what you pays for! If you are investing in a pickup for a retro fit, then go for a reputable brand and pay some decent money. Look for brands like Fishman, K&K, LR Baggs or Mi-Si. The Mi-Si pickups are very clever as they are active but use no 9v battery. They have a small capacitor fitted to the jackpin that you charge in 30 seconds on the mains, and it then remains charged for hours - very cool! If you are buying a uke with a pickup system already fitted, bear in mind that a great pickup will never turn a poor quality uke into something special - do the maths and work out whether it is too good to be true. A pickup system is realistically going to start at about £50 and may run into a cost over £100. If you see a ukulele with a £50 pickup for £60, the uke is almost certainly going to be junk!!

• The Amplifier is crucial - The sound you get from your uke is only going to be as good as the amplifier you are using. No matter how good the uke or the pickup, if you feed it into a poor amplifier you are wasting your time. It goes without saying that you want to look for an acoustic amplifier, and I personally use the Marshall AS50R Soloist amp. It has a great tone and is as good for filling a small hall as it is for home practice.

- DI Boxes - Some people swear by using a DI box that you plug into BEFORE plugging into the amp - it is basically an external pre-amplifier and EQ that aims to improve the sound going in to the amp and give it a more natural sound (piezos can sound a bit harsh and bright). I've never used one, and rely on my amp, but many do. I'd say, try before you buy.

Pickups are not for everyone, and if you are not planning to gig, probably not required at all. Retro fitting a pickup needs careful consideration as it involves drilling your uke in most cases - if in doubt, get it fitted by an expert.

Oh, and if you want to have some fun, once you

have a pickup you can put it through effects pedals to create some weird sounds, or create a rock uke! Kerrrrannnnggg!!!!

22. FINGERNAILS

Another common issue for those starting out with ukulele is how to treat their fingernails.

As I said earlier in the book, I don't really go in for playing the ukulele with a pick and prefer to strum with the fingertips. To get a sharper and louder sound, it really is essential that you have longer fingernails. If you want to get into finger picking, even longer still. So how do you go about it?

Well, firstly, we are ONLY talking about growing nails on the strumming hand. For accurate fretting, you want to keep the fingernails on that hand trimmed short.

For the strumming hand, well, the first step is really easy - don't cut or bite them!

For many though, that wont be enough as the nails need to be strong and not just long. First time nail growers may find their nails soft, bendy, or that they will easily break when strumming. This is not good news, and you can find that you are facing an uphill battle trying to keep the nails in good condition, whilst still trying to keep up your ukulele practice.

The following tips may help you in that regard. Male readers may wince at some of the tips as they make me sound like a beautician! Bear in mind, if you want to play fingerstyle with nails, you need to grow them AND look after them.

- Once grown, keeping them in good shape is essential - keep them sanded to the length you like for your playing style - do this religiously and carefully every day.
- Using nail conditioning creams and increasing your intake of Omega 3 (fatty fish oils) will improve the strength of your nails - plus it is good for you in many other ways!
- Don't grow them too long - this will depend on the shape of your fingers, but you only want them so long as to just protrude beyond the flesh of your fingertip - so it is the nail that hits the string first, not

skin. Keeping them the right length will reduce your chances of breaking them in other day-to-day things.

- Buff the flat face of the nail regularly with a buffing pad, and keep the cuticle pushed back, thereby helping keep the nail in good condition.

If you try the above (and persevere, it won't happen overnight) but are still having breakages or soft nails, you may need to consider an artificial solution

- Coat the nails with a clear nail varnish before playing. Some brands offer a super strength formula that is super tough! Feel free to go for a bright colour if you prefer – whatever floats your boat!
- Consider having a false nail tip or two added to the fingers you want to use for picking - sorry guys – a trip to the Nail bar!
- The ugly, but very workable solution employed by many guitarists is this - cut some single ply pieces of tissue paper to the sort of shape you want, about the sizes of

your fingernails. Cover the nail in a coat of clear varnish, and lay the tissue on to it making sure it protrudes beyond the edge of your actual nail and leave to dry. Build up layers of these sheets, letting each one dry hard each time. This will build up an ugly but strong artificial nail that sits on top of your own nail. All you need to do then is trim the tip to a nail shape.

Hopefully those tips will help you. To start off it takes patience and work, but it is worth it for that wonderful sound.

23. WHAT IS A K BRAND UKULELE?

As you develop your interest in the ukulele, you will find in your (many) web searches that you will find the term 'K Brand' when referring to ukuleles - but, what does that mean?

As explained earlier in this book, the ukulele, whilst European in origin, has it's roots deeply in the Hawaiian soil. The term K Brand really refers to the four main, hand made, and most well-known ukulele makers in Hawaii, namely, Kamaka, Kanile'a, KoAloha and Ko'olau. These brands are considered by many to be about the best around, using superb woods and age-old building techniques to create stunning instruments.

That said, there are actually a host of ukulele brands that begin with the letter K, including

Kala
Kawika
Kelii

Kohala

Many of these are not Hawaiian at all, in fact only Kelii is an actual hand made Hawaiian brand, with some of the others, such as Kala being made in the far east.

To further complicate matters, the term K Brand does something of a disservice to the wonderful Hawaiian uke manufacturer G-String, which are considered by many to be right up there with the big four K ukes.

Needless to say, if you are buying a genuine K Brand uke from those four (or a uke from G String) you are purchasing a high-end professional, hand made instrument that has not come from a mass production factory.

So, a little more about those top brands.

KAMAKA UKULELES

Kamaka ukes, with their distinctive double K logo on the headstock, were founded in 1916 by Samuel Kaialiilii Kamaka in Kaimuki, near Honolulu.

Kamaka are credited for inventing the pineapple shaped ukulele body, and are endorsed by some big ukulele names, including Jake Shimabukuro and George Harrison. They are also famed for their support of the disabled community, winning the Outstanding Employer for Persons with Disabilities award.

They manufacture 9 models of ukulele in a variety of sizes.

KANILE'A UKULELES

Kanile'a ukes are a more modern brand, but made on Hawaii to similar exacting hand made standards by Joe and Kristen in Kaneohe.

Joe started playing uke at school and started training to be a master luthier in 1990, and in the last 20 years has built up an enviable reputation for quality instruments.

They offer a large range of models, with some special finishes and bracing systems.

KOALOHA UKULELES

Koaloha ukes are hand crafted in Honolulu by Alvin Okami, who actually started his career as a singer!

Alvin started his manufacturing business in 1981, and now make a large range of high quality ukes in a variety of styles including the unique Pineapple Sunday, considered by many to be one of the best 'stand out' ukes on the market.

KO'OLAU UKULELES

Ko'olau started in 1979 as Kitakis Stringed Instruments, based in Wahiawa, Hawaii. The business expanded, and changed its name to

Ko'olau, named after the mountain range on the eastern edge of the volcano on the island of O'ahu.

The company started in the early years making a small number of hand made ukes and mandolins, but mainly focussed on repairs to instruments. In the 1990's and the resurgence in ukulele popularity and the business expanded to the large range of expertly built, hand made ukes available to this day. Ko'olau are also responsible for the Pono (non hand made) line of mid level ukuleles

G STRING UKULELES

G String ukuleles, as I say above, are the honorary K Brand uke - honorary because sadly their name does not begin with a K, but they are right up there in the quality stakes!

They are a small company located in the Hilawa valley on the island of O'ahu, with a smaller number of ukes in the product range, but expertly built, and, of course, offering bespoke services. Started in

1993 in a single garage they have quickly built a huge reputation.

24. ADVANCED STRUMMING TECHNIQUES

As you will have read in this book, I do encourage new ukulele players to try not to be swayed by fancy strums, and concentrate on mastering a simple strum and getting the rhythm right. That said, to spruce up your ukulele playing, you may want to consider adding some frills to your playing as you progress.

I list below some basic guides to some other strum techniques that you might want to consider trying. There are no hard and fast rules - try to develop your own style!

Firstly, before we get into the advanced tricks, if you are an absolute beginner, your strum may simply consist of (in a 4/4 time song) Down - Down - Down - Down - and you probably think it sounds a little dull. You may have moved on to a Down-Up, Down-Up, Down-Up, Down-Up, which adds a bit more life, but can sound rather like an Oom-Pah band! So before you move on to investigate the tricks below, try some more work on your strum patterns. Mix it up a little, and try new things out

How about - Down, Down-Up, Down, Down-Up - (this is very simple and creates a kind of country music style)? As I say, there are no rules!

Also, work on the hammer ons, vibratos and pull offs that I discussed in an earlier chapter.

ARPEGGIOS

This fancy name is the term given to the very simple technique of plucking the individual notes of a chord instead of strumming them. Try to replace the odd strum with a quick finger pick of the individual strings one after the other. This can be done in the simplest way by simply picking the strings in order from top to bottom or bottom to top, but you can add more flavour to your sound by picking the strings out of order - try some different patterns, but always picking all the strings, and keeping your picking pattern in time with the music

(as a direct replacement to the strum)

CHUNKING

This is a nice ukulele technique (also known as Chucking) which punctuates your strumming rhythm with a staccato muting of the strings - very effective to get a chugging rhythm going, and super effective in reggae or ska music. It gets its name from the chunk chunka chunk chunka sound it creates.

Very simple to do, but its more tricky to master into a steady rhythm so will require practice.

To chunk on your ukulele, the immediate split second after your strum, mute the strings with the fleshy underside of your hand (I tend to use the fat part of the base of my thumb). This immediately kills and deadens the chord notes you have just played. Try muting first on every strum to get a feel for it, but you will create more of a grooving rhythm if you alternate your mutes to every other strum, or trying other patterns.

DEAD STRUMMING

This is the action of muting all the strings with your fretting hand (by lightly holding your fingers across them), and strumming the ukulele as normal. This just creates a clicking percussive sound which you can use in certain points in a song to create a beat. No notes are sounded, just the sound of your nails on the strings. Very effective in certain songs, and sounds great when you then immediately move into a chord and the music comes back to life!

SPLIT STROKE

This is a fancy strum technique made famous by George Formby. It's quite easy to describe, but rather more difficult to master!

The simple technique is to strum a chord down wards, then, still holding the chord shape, immediately pluck the A then the G string before your next strum. The key is to use the plucks in time with the beat of your strumming. When done very quickly, this is often called "The Shake".

FAN STROKE

The fan stroke has its roots in Spanish flamenco guitar playing, and adds a real zing to your strumming. Rather than just strumming the string downwards with your index finger, the fan stroke uses ALL of your fingers, rather like you were dragging a comb down across the strings - with each finger catching each of the strings in succession.

For all of the above, YouTube is a superb tutor aid, and you will find countless videos showing these techniques now that you know what they are. As I say though, DO try to find your OWN style, and keep in mind that there is no real right or wrong way to strum. Do try to liven up your playing though, and work with differing beats to your strumming to add a bit of flavour to your sound. Try adding a plucked note here and there, or hammering on and off of a single finger in a chord as you strum to bring a bit more life to it. Experiment!

Good luck!

25. WHEN SHOULD I CHANGE MY STRINGS?

Firstly, the answer to the question does of course depend on how often you play your ukulele, and how aggressive your playing style is. Clearly, somebody who plays their uke for ten hours a day EVERY day will need to consider a string change more often than a player who has a light strum on high days and holidays only!

Ukulele strings are made of nylon, or a nylon type substance, and as such stand up to oils and grease from fingertips far better than steel strings you find on an electric our acoustic folk guitar. Any guitarists reading this will know how quickly their strings go "off". To start with, you can see them deteriorate as they take on a dull look. On my guitar, when I am playing regularly, I can end up changing strings every couple of weeks!

For a ukulele, generally speaking you will find that nylon strings last much longer than this, perhaps even months.

As for the ideal time to change them, you should probably consider a change if any of the points below apply:

1. Are there any nicks, flat spots or grooves cut into the strings? This can occur from constant pressure on the frets, or, as the string stretches, as the string is retuned the part that was resting in the nut becomes visible between the nut and the tuning peg - the tell tale sign are little horizontal lines across the string. These can affect tuning, and will eventually break.

2. Are you having trouble holding your tuning? - Whilst uke strings can be a real pain to keep in tune when they are new because of the stretching they undergo, when they have stretched to their optimum, they really should stay in tune when left alone. If you have some seasoned strings like this but are finding that tuning is going off, or intonation is a problem, you should consider a string change.

3. Do they just sound dull? As ukulele strings age, they will eventually lose their tonal qualities and you

may find that your uke just doesn't sound very bright any more - again - time for a string change.

String changes are not difficult, and ukulele strings are not expensive, so give it a go!

26. UKULELE WOODS AND THEIR INFLUENCE ON SOUND

In your hunt to purchase a ukulele you will have noticed that there are a variety of different wood types you can buy - but how do they affect the sound?

In this guide I will give you my views on how the wood used in a ukulele affects the sound. This is in respect (in the main) of solid top instruments, not laminates. Laminates do vary by wood type, but the differences tend to be more in respect of how good a quality laminate it is. Solid woods though can have a big impact on the sound of the instrument.

Firstly, there is no right and wrong when it comes to wood types, and there is certainly no "best" wood. All woods differ and they sound they make has also got to be something you like the sound of. What sounds best to your ears may be different to mine. That said, I list below some of the main wood types you will encounter when ukulele shopping and their common characteristics.

MAHOGANY

One of the most common woods in ukulele making, it has a reasonable grain finish providing good looks, but provides a good balance between the bright trebly sounds the ukulele is famous for, whilst beefing up the bass sounds a little too. Also projects sound well with good volume. It's also cheaper than many other tonewoods, and as such provides, in my opinion, the best value for quality.

KOA

Koa is a Hawaiian hardwood, and a ukulele wood held in very high esteem in those islands. The wood is beautiful to look at with amazing grains (particularly the curly variety), and provides a sound that suits the ukulele perfectly. Very sweet sounding and warm. Loud rich, and used in the finest ukuleles, but very expensive. Koa instrument prices show the premium!

CEDAR

A common, reddish soft wood often used in acoustic guitars, cedar has a plain finish, and provides a very warm sound, evenly distributed amongst the strings. To my ear, a little too muddy sounding for the ukulele for which I appreciate a bit more treble, but a good wood nonetheless.

SPRUCE

A very common, pale yellow wood used in guitar manufacture. Now seen on many cheaper ukuleles on the top only (usually with rosewood or mahogany backs and sides). It is a tough wood that makes for excellent strong soundboards and the Sitka variety is characterised by a very bright and rich tone, with less of the bass rounding that Mahogany provides. They are also very loud woods, but a touch TOO bright for my ears. Engelmann spruce is a slightly mellower version that is often used in classical instruments.

MAPLE

A hard, resilient wood that is often chosen for its dramatic looks, particularly flamed or spalted woods that are stunning to look at. It provides a very very bright tone on the ukulele.

MANGO

A beautiful looking, orange wood with beautiful grain, that is used increasingly as a more sustainable wood choice (as Mango is a fruit tree, the wood is harvested after the tree is no longer efficiently producing fruit, and is then replanted). Mango provides a warm yet bright tone, similar to walnut.

OTHERS

The woods above are amongst the most common you will find, but there are many others, each with differing properties (too many to go into in this beginners guide!) including Bubinga, Acacia,

Lacewood and Myrtle. If you are going into the exotic wood direction, speak to a maker and ask opinions on sound, or better still, play before you buy.

27. DO I NEED A CASE?

This is a question I see asked a lot by those starting out and considering their first ukulele purchase - do you need a case for your uke?

It is, of course, personal choice, and depends very much on the cost of the instrument and what you are planning to do with it.

Cases come in three main varieties, hard cases, soft shell cases, and soft cases. Each offer different levels of protection for the ukulele, and come at different price points.

HARD CASES

Hard ukulele cases, as the name suggests are completely hard and solid and, generally speaking, provide the best quality protection. They are either made of a vinyl / tolex covered plywood (at the cheaper end of the scale) or from moulded polycarbonate or aluminium at the upper end. They are usually padded inside with a fur lining to protect the finish of the uke. They tend also to have a small accessory chamber inside, and some may have humidification systems. They secure with metal clasps, sometimes with a lock on one of them.

Bear in mind that a cheap hard case, made of plywood, may actually be a worse investment than a good padded case. Such cases really only provide a bit of protection against knocks and will not withstand being crushed or trodden on. If you plan to put your uke in a coach luggage hold, or on an aircraft, I would recommend a good quality ABS Polycarbonate or aluminium case as it will stand up better to being squashed.

I use a hard shell ABS case made by Gator, and Calton and Hiscox also make some of the best around.

SOFT SHELL CASES / POD CASES

This is the halfway house case - it is a soft case, usually made of a padded nylon material but have stiffened rigid sides to provide some extra protection from squashing (though not a lot). They are certainly a great case for packing the uke in the trunk of a car where some other light luggage is placed on top. Soft shell cases are light, cheaper than good quality hard cases (though often more expensive than the cheap hard shell plywood cases) and tend to come with other extras that hard shell cases don't, such as extra accessory pockets with zips and shoulder straps.

SOFT CASES

This is the lower end type of case and is really only a gig bag for transportation. They are again made of padded nylon (the cheapest having the least amount of padding) and offer no rigidity. As such, they are super light, cheap, and great for carrying your uke about and avoiding it being knocked or scratched, but not a great deal more.

So which case should you buy - well as I said in the opening, it depends on the cost of the uke (or how important it is to you) and what you plan to do with it. Regardless of the ukulele, if you only ever plan to use it at home and when not being played, keep it in a safe place for storage, even for an expensive uke, a soft case may be all you need. If you are considering transporting your ukulele, or take it gigging, if the uke is of any value at all, you should think about moving up the quality scale. For air travel, you should only consider a hard case that has been rated for air travel and bear in mind this can cost a serious amount of money.

Personally speaking, I would highly recommend some sort of case for whatever your uke. Even if you are buying a cheap entry-level ukulele, look for a soft case to allow you to carry it around to all those clubs, pubs and gigs you are going to be trying out! If you have spent a little bit more on a uke, I personally would only consider a hardshell ABS type case, its all I really trust, and its a one off purchase that I always know is available to me, whether I travel or not.

As final thought, if you are buying a decent ukulele

mail order, if you call the store and order a case at the same time, not only might you be able to negotiate a discount, you can ask them to ship the ukulele inside the case - meaning added protection when shipping.

28. FINGER STRETCHING EXERCISES

If you have just started with your ukulele, you may well be in pain! As mentioned in the chapter on sore fingers, this is a natural reaction for a new player and something that you will have to go through. I thought though I would write a longer chapter with some tips on how to speed the process along.

When you start to play uke, your body, and in particular, the fingers of your fretting hand, will not be used to creating the chord shapes you are trying to get them in to. In fact, some chord shapes you may find downright impossible because your fingers just wont seem to bend or reach the required frets. Worry not; it DOES get easier with practice practice practice.

What you need to achieve is a muscle memory in your fingers so that the shapes you are trying to perform come naturally and easily. Much the same as a pro tennis player practices their serves over and over until their arm gets into a "groove" they can repeat easily, you need to train your fingers, muscles and tendons to start forming common shapes and reaching in ways your hand has never needed to before. So, some tips to help you along, and relieve the cramps and pains!

Non-ukulele exercises

Firstly, lets look at some exercises you can do without even having your ukulele to hand. During your day, concentrate on doing repetitions of spreading your fingers wide as far as they will go, then crunched into a fist - repeat this over and over and over.

Try holding your hand with the palm facing you and bend your forefinger down trying to reach as far down your palm as you can. Repeat with the other fingers and, again, repeat this over and over.

Some people also report success by using a stress ball, (or a tennis ball) and squeezing and massaging it during the day.

Ukulele exercises

The best exercises though are those that you practice on the ukulele. Try these AS WELL AS practising your chord shapes and before long you will build up strength and the ability to stretch those fingers.

BASIC EXERCISE

Holding your uke practice doing some note runs on the strings. Start on the G string, and fret at the first with your forefinger, then the second with your middle finger, the third with your ring finger and the fourth with your pinky. Then move on to the C string, and then the same on the E and A strings. When you get to the fourth fret of the A string, do the same thing in reverse. This is basic fretting practice putting the most obvious fingers on the most obvious frets. Plucking each note will also give you some note recognition practice. Ensure your fretting on each note is clean, using your fingertip perpendicular to the fingerboard and squarely between the frets.

When you are starting out I would suggest running this practice about 10 times up and down the notes at the start of every practice session.

INTERMEDIATE EXERCISE

If you find the above nice and easy, you can step it up a notch

a) Using just your first and middle finger, start on the G string fretting at the first with the forefinger then the third with your middle finger (hopping over and missing the second fret), then move on to the C, E an A strings, then run it back in reverse.

b) Using just your first and ring finger do the same exercise but this time stretching your ring finger directly to the fourth fret on each string, working up through the strings, then coming back again in reverse.

c) Using just your first and pinky, repeat as above,

but this time using your pinky to stretch to the 5th string.

For all of the above - again practice each 10 or 20 times before you start your ukulele session

MORE ADVANCED EXERCISES

There is really no limit to where you can go with advanced exercises - you want to try to create something repetitive that REALLY stretches those fingers!

I use the following pattern that really does work those finger muscles.

Holding your uke, put your fore finger on the E string at the first fret, and your middle finger on the A string first fret. Strum twice, then move your middle finger up one fret to the second (leaving the forefinger on the E string at the first) and strum twice again. Then move that middle finger up another one and repeat. Keep going, keeping the forefinger anchored at the 1st fret on the E string, moving the middle finger up the A string a fret at a time. Then do it back down in reverse and repeat over and over. I can personally get my middle finger to the 5th fret when my forefinger is anchored at the first on the E string.

Then move on to your ring finger. Do exactly the same thing, keeping that forefinger anchored at the first on the E string, but move the ring finger up the frets of the A string one at a time strumming as you go. I can get my ring finger to the 6th doing it this way.

Finally, do the same for the pinky, which should be able to go a little bit further (I can JUST about get my pinky to the 7th!)

The above is a great advanced stretch technique that should help you pick out those more difficult notes with ease

I hope these help you - there is no easy quick fix for hand cramps - practice practice practice!

29. THE UKULELE BOOM

It is now abundantly clear to anyone but those with their heads in the sand that the ukulele has recently seen a huge upswing in popularity around the globe. I find that it is now quite difficult to go through a day watching or listening to popular culture without hearing a ukulele at some point. An increasing number of pop artists, television advertisements and trailers are choosing the uke as the instrument of choice in their musical background. Social Media is bursting with new ukulele players looking for advice and ukulele clubs are springing up all over the place around the globe. I have spoken to a number of musical instrument retailers recently and they tell me that they can't get hold of ukuleles quickly enough to meet customer demand. How long will it last and will the ukulele bubble burst?

Now it may seem odd for to introduce a negative into a book that aims to promote playing the uke, but the very short answer to the question is, yes, probably! Like everything, the popularity will start to wane at some point, but there is no need to worry, it won't go away. Music never does. (And if it ever does, take me out in the yard and shoot me – a world without music would be a sad, sad place).

All sorts of music tastes and interests come and go in popularity over the years, but they never die, and sure enough they will come back again at some point in the future. It was ever thus. To understand where we are today with the ukulele, we need to go back in time to the last big upswing for this plucky little instrument.

So let us roll back the clock to the 1930's and 40's and we find that the ukulele was BIG! HUGE in fact! These were the days before television networks and pop charts, but the ukulele was the staple instrument for many music hall entertainers. Cliff Edwards, Roy Smeck, George Formby are names you may have heard of, but there were countless others who, at some point in their act they would grab a uke to sing, play and entertain the masses. In keeping with the happy nature of the instrument, many, like Formby used the uke in comic and whimsical songs, but as many played the uke to accompany serious and touching songs, using its simple voice to bring a note of sadness to a performance. It was everywhere. Music stores on both sides of the Atlantic were full of ukes, and not guitars. A child's first instrument was most likely a cheap ukulele, perhaps made of Bakelite or later, brittle brightly coloured plastic. Then, like today, the public was exposed to an significant amount of ukulele music on the radio, in the movies and on stage. Also like today, when a member of the public picked up an instrument they quickly realised that it was a fairly simple instrument to get to grips with, benefited from being cheap and portable and was a huge amount of fun to play. Looking back to the present day and we see that those attributes haven't changed one bit, only the style and the fashion of the players.

I appreciate that some of you may look back on those early artists and cringe or exclaim that they are not your 'thing'. Some people actually don't like the link that the ukulele has with the likes of George Formby at all and actively try to avoid it coming up in conversation. Whilst many people do still enjoy that style of music, I am sure that the younger players today may find it 'old fashioned' compared to the current crop of artists today who are bringing the uke into their compositions, like Beirut, Noah And The Whale and Eddie Vedder. You may find, when playing a ukulele around those of the older generation, that you get ribbed by them asking that you 'play us some George Formby' or similar retorts. I have a healthy respect for Mr Formby, for sure, but I have to admit that I don't sit listening to his music on a daily basis.

But the thing is, those guys were actually no different to the artists of today. Those guys WERE the hit artists of their day. Formby and Edwards were, literally, megastars and as such what they sang and played had a huge influence on the general public. These people were the equivalent of the multi million selling hit artists of today. To put it another way, George Formby was the Jay Z of his day (now there is an image, Jay Z playing When I'm Cleaning Windows...shudder.) George, Cliff and Roy may sound old fashioned now, but back then it was absolutely bang on the moment (and the money!). Were you alive in those days with even a passing interest in music, if you play the ukulele today I'd wager you would have played it then and talked about it the way you do now. In fact, those artists careers were so big, that the ukulele upswing of that period was actually much bigger than the one we have now.

So, what happened? Why did the ukulele fall out of favour in those days? Several things contributed to the decline, namely the advent of TV, Rock & Roll and a significant widening in media outlets and musical tastes. The old time artists who principally plied their trade on the music hall stages became somewhat marginalised and the new younger record buying public wanted nothing but rock and roll (note, Elvis played a ukulele, but for the children of the 50's, a skiffle guitar was where it was at!). The world then went though a period of pop, rock, metal, dance and a million other music styles that came and went, and the ukulele just got lost in all the noise. But it didn't die, far from it. In fact, in the background there remained a faithful contingent that continued to play and of course, in the islands of Hawaii, it never went away at all.

We now fast forward back to more recent years and we find that the ukulele has started to find its voice heard on certain popular music tracks. This hasn't been a case, like the last upswing in the 40's and 50's of the ukulele dominating the charts and the music shops, but it was quietly growing, being picked up by artists of high standing in the modern music business. Elvis Costello, Bruce Springsteen, Amanda Palmer, Stephin Merritt and others started appearing in gigs with a uke in hand, or including the instrument on record. Music generally also seems to have taken a turn, in recent years, to a folkier style, which the ukulele naturally fits in with. Whilst many of the 'nu folk' artists may not (yet!) have included the ukulele in their work, artists like Fleet Foxes, Laura Marling and Mumford & Sons have achieved huge success with a folky, acoustic sound that suits this instrument. The musical landscape has shifted a little. People started talking about the ukulele more, looking for shops that could sell them one and searching out anything they could find on the Internet to learn more about the instrument. Forums, clubs and blogs started appearing at an incredible rate, and judging by the membership numbers on the main ukulele discussion forums, a massive number of people out there now wanted to play. Music shops started dedicating one shelf, then whole walls to stocking ukuleles in their stores, with new outlets setting up to sell nothing but the uke. The upswing was in full 'swing'.

In a single hour-long programme on British television recently I watched selected highlights of a popular UK Folk Festival. I saw about six or seven acts in total and counted five ukuleles during the programme. That's a pretty good hit rate! (Plus, one was an exotic looking five string!). Amanda Palmer of the Dresden Dolls, a band who describe themselves as a 'Brechtian Punk Cabaret', and with who you would never associate the ukulele, released an EP of ukulele songs and now regularly gigs with a uke despite her earlier career being led by piano which she plays so well. She then went on to release a concept album Evelyn Evelyn based on a fictional pair of conjoined twins who play, you guessed it, a ukulele. Eddie Vedder, lead singer with the rock band Pearl Jam released a whole album of ukulele tracks much to the bemusement of some of his established fan base. The album featured some new songs written just for the instrument, and some covers of his earlier Pearl

Jam tracks given a complete makeover on the little instrument. It went on to sell very well, and saw Vedder performing tracks on Letterman accompanied only by himself on a tenor ukulele. These two releases are not examples of what started the upswing but are examples of artists taking advantage of it. Vedder has been a fan of the ukulele for his whole life but would he have had success releasing a ukulele album in 1995? I suspect not.

So behind the world of celebrity it started to grow, and grow very quickly. For the general public the same attributes that got people hooked on the uke in the 1930's still hold true today. They can be cheap to buy, they are easy to get started with, they are portable and they are tremendous fun. What wasn't to like

This current upswing is different though, as we live in different times. I personally can't see the ukulele ever reaching the heady heights it achieved in the 30's and 40's again, there is too much competition in the music field and too many music styles out there. But I think I prefer that. Music is music, and I personally prefer balance and variety rather than one instrument dominating the whole world. It's likely to be an instrument that you will continue to see and hear regularly, that new bands seek to try out and include on an album once in a while. We can expect to find more unusual collaborations that fuse the ukulele with different types of music as new players experiment more with it. A prime example of that is a video you can look at by searching for Jessica Latshaw, in particular her video on the New York City Subway that sees an impromptu uke performance in an R&B style, accompanied by a stranger playing the congas to a thrilled bunch of strangers that just happened to be travelling on the same train. That sort of experimentation may actually serve to keep the interest going longer or even indefinitely, and that is no bad thing.

All of that said, as a humble non-celebrity, does any of this really matter to me? Perhaps not. At the end of the day I play the ukulele because I enjoy it and it makes me happy. If the world turned off the uke tomorrow, this player wouldn't. Once you are a player, it's no longer about the fashion of the day. Some established ukulele players choose to 'pooh-

pooh' the new fad they see with younger players, and I don't think that is particularly fair. They claim that they will put their ukes down as quickly as they picked them up, that they are not taking it seriously. I take issue with that. Whatever it takes in getting people playing music (on any instrument, whether ukulele or otherwise) is OK in my book and should never be sniffed at. We should remember that those young players who start today may turn out to be the grandparent who passes on a treasured ukulele to a grandchild some fifty years hence and, in turn, starts another generation on the road with the Uke!

Enjoy this ukulele boom whilst it's here, but don't forget, your uke is for life!

30. BASIC THEORY PT1 – NOTES

From this point on in the book are one or two more chapters dealing with the same subject and they represent some of the absolute basics that I think it would be helpful for a beginner to try to understand. Firstly then, let's take a look at the notes on a ukulele.

As you will probably know by now, the strings on a standard tuned ukulele are tuned to G,C,E and A (with the G on the string nearest the ceiling, and A on the string nearest the floor). If the strings are plucked without touching the neck, these are the notes that will ring, as the strings are being played in what is called 'open'.

But of course, the neck of your ukulele is covered with frets to allow you to change the notes. When you fret a string on the ukulele you shorten the length, which in turn changes the way it vibrates and makes it ring a sound that is higher in pitch. The frets on a ukulele are spaced precisely such that playing a single string and ascending up the neck of the instrument one fret at a time will raise the note that is played by a 'half step' in musical terms (the equivalent of moving to the next key on a piano keyboard). Knowing this, and that moving up each fret moves you up a half step in the scale, by knowing the notes your open strings are tuned to, you should be able to work out any note on the whole of the ukulele fingerboard.

So how do we work up the note scale? Well, as you probably know, major notes in music are named as A, B, C, D, E, F, and G. It does however get a little more complicated as we have sharps and flats, and these represent intermediate notes between some of these major notes.

The sequence actually runs like this:

A - A#/Bb - B - C - C#/Db - D - D#/Eb - E - F - F#/Gb - G - G#/Ab - and then back to the next A.

This run of notes from that lower A to the next one up (or down!) is called an Octave.

The '#' symbol above means a sharp note and the 'b' means a flat. They are named together as they are essentially the same note and depending on your convention you will see both around - the A# plays the same as a Bb as it is the same thing.

But hang on, you are asking, why are there no sharps/flats between some of the notes, like between the B and C and the E and F? Well, due to the mechanics and the mathematics of the way music works, they don't exist! If you can picture a piano keyboard, the black keys represent the sharps and flats. If you look, the black keys don't actually appear between each and every white key, in some cases the white keys are directly next to each other with no black key between them. These are the keys that represent those notes above that don't have a sharp or a flat.

So, now you know the theory of how the notes run through a musical octave, if you take your ukulele and look at the G string (the one nearest the ceiling!) - using the list of notes above, you now know that the first fret will play you a G#/Ab, the second fret an A, the third fret an A#/Bb, the fourth fret a B and so on. You can apply this to the other strings as well, and using the sequence work out any note at any fret on the ukulele!

If you are feeling brave you could try to memorise them all and many players can do this, and have the great ability to find any note anywhere on the ukulele. This brings many advantages in composing melodies and forming chords further up the neck of the instrument on the fly. For beginners though, I wouldn't worry about trying to do that straight away. I would, however, suggest that there is great merit in you learning every note on the ukulele up to the first four or five frets.

31. UKULELE ACTION

Earlier I explained about ukulele setup and intonation as being things critical to a ukulele that plays well and in tune. As part of that process, we dealt with something called 'action' and how that is part of the setup. Action in itself, unless at the extremes of low or high, is not necessarily something that can cause a problem with tuning, and some players have very personal preferences on how they like their ukulele action. That said it's something that you, as an instrument owner should understand and be confident in adjusting.

The term 'action' means the way the strings of the ukulele relate to the fingerboard over which they pass. That is to say, the angle and height of the strings in relation to the straight fingerboard.

You will hear of poor action as being either 'high' or 'low', and they each create their own problems when adjusted to the extremes.

1. A high action affects the playability of the

instrument (the way the uke feels and how easy and fast it is to play) as well as the intonation of the instrument and tuning accuracy as we discussed earlier

2. Low action will most likely cause buzzing, or in extreme cases, the muting of the whole string, as the strings are too close to the frets. In the extreme cases it may actually have the effect of shortening the string if, for example, the string is 'bottoming out' on one of the frets and in such cases the string will sound muted or dull.

In respect of the former, if playability is bad enough this will lead to aching sore fingers. A high string simply requires more effort to push it down to the fret, and more distance to travel. This can cause cramp and also significantly slows down how quickly and cleanly you can change notes in melodies or chords.

Like it or not, a stringed instrument is a mathematical thing. That taut string requires itself to be as parallel as possible to the fingerboard in order that when fretted, the corresponding fret creates the right note. If you imagine a very high bridge, the string will get closer and closer along its length to the fingerboard as it approaches the nut. In other words, it is the hypotenuse of a long, very thin triangle. Raise the bridge too high, and your mathematics knowledge will tell you that the hypotenuse will lengthen. The fret placement relies on the length of the string between nut and bridge measured in a straight line to be fixed and accurate in relation to the neck. Raise the bridge, you lengthen the hypotenuse and throw out the mathematics! The result is that the notes that ring at certain fret positions will be out of tune.

A high nut can create the same thing on it's own, but more commonly will manifest it's problem in tuning at the first and second frets. A string leaving a high nut when fretted at the first requires the string to be pulled down too far from it's horizontal and this too lengthens that hypotenuse and throws out the tuning.

But that is straying back into intonation, which we have already talked about, and it is important to know that you can have a high action without intonation problems.

So what makes the 'right' action? Well that depends entirely on your own playing style, but mine currently measure between 1/8 and 3/16 of an inch between the string and the top of the crown of the 12th fret.

Assuming you don't have intonation problems and your ukulele is in tune all over the neck to raise or lower the action requires, typically, an adjustment to the bridge saddle of the ukulele. Raising the bridge by placing a thin shim of wood underneath the saddle of the ukulele, or lowering it by sanding the saddle base is the usual way to adjust action. Bear in mind that the adjustments need to be extremely minor if you are to avoid creating intonation problems that were not there in the first place.

There are many times when a player may find he wants to adjust the action of a uke. Old vintage instruments do change, bend and warp over time as the tension of the strings over many years has served to pull the bridge up towards the nut and in doing so has warped or stretched the natural wood material the instrument is made from. Alternatively if you fit an under saddle pickup to a ukulele you will, naturally raise the height of the bridge saddle as it is now sitting on thin strip of the pickup piezo element, and as such will need to be sanded back a little.

You may also want to experiment in playing slide ukulele, and for that you will want to raise your action high at the bridge, or preferably, at the nut with a replacement nut block in order that you don't have issues with your slide hitting the frets (slide guitar and ukulele means that the frets become redundant and the notes are picked out by holding a metal or glass 'slide' against the strings to act like a moveable fret).

But for general playing, the trick is to get the strings as low as possible without killing the tone by being too close to the body and fingerboard, or worse still buzzing on the frets themselves. With experience you will learn to find the sweet spot that suits your ukuleles tone and your own playing style.

If in doubt, speak to a guitar tech or luthier!

32. THE DREADED E CHORD

Despite me regularly pointing out to people that the ukulele is a fairly simple instrument to start to learn, I am commonly told that there is one particular chord that causes untold problems to beginners and more advanced players alike. The dreaded E chord. (cue dramatic music, Psycho style...)

It's a shame really, because the E is a lovely sounding chord, and it's also a really common chord, so as you build up a song repertoire you will find that you struggle to avoid using it. Firstly, the correct advice from me is, of course, that any instrument requires practice and dedication, and if you try to find a way around it, you are only leaving yourself with a problem further down the line. As such it is probably better to just learn how to play it. Yes, the E Chord is a toughie. If you take a look at your ukulele chord chart (one is available for free on the Got A Ukulele website) you will find the standard chord shape for the E chord. It is numbered as 4442.

To play E in this way, you put your first finger on

the A string at the second fret, and then need to cram your second and third fingers onto the other strings at the fourth fret, or use a finger to barre those remaining strings without muting the A string. For beginners, it is awkward, it hurts, and is just plain difficult, particularly when trying to effect a smooth transition to or from other chords, and many new players who master the act of holding the chord really struggle to move to it from another chord very quickly. There isn't a ukulele god out there deliberately trying to make things difficult for you, it's just the way the construction of the chord works on a ukulele fretboard. An E chord on a guitar is an easy chord to play as it has the benefit of extra strings that come in to play, but in equal measure there are plenty of guitar chords that are much harder to play than they are on a ukulele!

One way that someone recommended me practicing the E chord is as follows.

First, fret a Bm chord, using a barre on the second fret with your first finger, and using your ring finger to stretch over to fret the G string at the fourth fret with the fingertip (4222). This is slightly tricky, but considerably easier than the E, so get comfortable strumming that chord. Now simply roll the fingertip of that ring finger down so it too starts to barre the C and the A strings at the fourth fret, whilst leaving your forefinger across the second fret. The beauty of this is that the first finger is already in place for the A string at the second fret – it doesn't need to move at all, and the rolling action of flattening your ring finger turns the 4222 into 4442.

As I say, it would be wrong of me to tell you to avoid it. It's a chord that you really do need to learn, and you need to accept that this one will simply take more practice to get right so I hope the above tip works for you. There are, however, some other alternatives to the standard E that you may find easier to play.

You could try to play it 1402 (ie G string at the first fret, C string at the fourth, E string open, and A string at the second) which many ukulele players recommend as an alternative but you may also find that method a bit of a stretch. It does however sound particularly great because you are creating two E notes in the chord and it helps the chord ring.

My own favourite alternative to the standard E is to

do a 'fourth fret lay across' (I know, I know, that sounds like a gymnastic technique or an obscure chess move). This involves using your index finger to barre across all strings at the 4th fret and using your ring finger to hold the A string at the 7th fret. This is written as 4447, and whilst it's a bit of a leap in distance from the nut for chord changes, it's not too difficult to actually finger and sounds very nice. You could even try barring those first three strings at the fourth fret by laying your thumb across them – unconventional perhaps, and again, more difficult to make the transition to and from the chord, but many play this way as it suits them. Give it a try

If you really want to cheat, depending on the song you could try replacing the E chord altogether with an E7 chord (1202), or even an Em chord (0432). This is a complete cheat and not correct musically, and it won't necessarily work on all songs. Some songs work better with the E7, some with the Em, and some with neither and you will have to trust your own ears to find what works. By all means try those, but try to find room in your practice schedule to working on the actual E. It's horrible to hold when starting out, but worth it.

33. DEVICES TO TUNE YOUR UKULELE

Earlier I told you how to tune your ukulele and gave some general recommendations on how to tune. This section aims to look at the options in a little more detail, which you may find helpful for those days your tuner battery dies. (Trust me, it will happen to you at some point..)

The ukulele has four strings, in most cases tuned to G, C, E and A, so to tune the uke you need at the very least, a reference pitch for just one of those strings, though ideally all of them.

USING A REFERENCE PITCH

This requires you to tune the ukulele by ear against a single, or set of known notes that match the GCEA tuning. This could be from the notes on a piano or another instrument that you know is in tune. Pick out the notes, and then tune your uke so the plucked string matches the reference note.

A traditional way of doing this is by purchasing a tuning fork or a set of ukulele pitch pipes. But hang on, if I only have one tuning fork, how can I tune the other strings? This is a handy tip for a beginner to know that will be a real help if you are tuning during a gig or without a tuner.

To do this, use a G tuning fork, and tune the G-string to the correct pitch by ear. If you then hold the G-string at the 5th fret and pluck you will hear a C note. Use this as the reference pitch for the next string, the C-string so you are tuning the next string to the first one you worked on. Then pluck the C-string at the fourth fret and you will hear an E. Use this as a reference pitch for the next string, the E-string. Similarly, pluck the E-string at the fifth fret, and this will give you an A reference to tune the A string.

Be aware that for an absolute beginner, tuning by ear in this way can be quite difficult to master. That said, I would however urge all beginners to try to do this as much as possible as learning the notes by ear is excellent practice and will help you in playing and understanding how the strings sound, and when they sound bad! The above sequence of tuning one string from another is only one pattern and when you learn the notes on a ukulele you should be able to spot how to create another string note from the one you know is in tune in a variety of different ways.

TUNING DEVICES

There is a huge range of ukulele tuning devices available on the market. If you have an electric uke, you can use pretty much any tuner that is designed for guitar by connecting the uke to the tuner with a guitar cable. Some of those tuners have microphones built in so no cable is required.

In more recent years though, the clip on tuner has really boomed in music stores. These were developed some years ago, and as I recall, Intellitouch were one of the first to market, initially developed for orchestra players to tune violins and the like with little fuss. They were however quite expensive, so the good news is that the prices have come right down and there is a whole range of them out there for only a few pounds.

Clip on tuners (usually) work by attaching to the headstock with a sprung clip, and the device senses the vibration in the instrument when a string is plucked. The note played is displayed in either LED lights (usually red for out of tune and green for in tune) or Letters, or even better, an LCD display showing a virtual needle. Pluck the string, see what the device is telling you (are you sharp or flat) and adjust until the correct reading is shown. Simple! Bear in mind though that clip on tuners tend to be a problem for beginners who are trying to tune a ukulele that is completely out. They really only work best when the ukulele is generally in the right ballpark for fine tuning, as a string that is miles away from where it should be can tend to confuse the electronics. As such, before using a clip on tuner it is a good idea to make sure the ukulele is as close as you can get it by ear.

They are though, quick and easy to use, light, and can be left clipped to the headstock whilst you are playing to give you a constant reference to whether you are in tune – particularly helpful when you have new strings on the instrument. As I say, there are plenty out there, but I personally use a Cherub, a Kala, and more recently a Snark, which is without a doubt my favourite model and is astoundingly accurate.

I would recommend all beginners purchase a clip on tuner in order that you can get tuned quickly when required, but as I say, urge you to put some practice in to tuning by ear - a valuable skill to learn for a life ahead with the ukulele.

34. LOW G TUNING AND RE-ENTRANT TUNING

You should now know that Soprano, Concert and Tenor ukuleles are best and most normally tuned in GCEA tuning. That is to say that the string nearest the floor (string 1) is tuned to A, then moving up towards the ceiling, the following strings are tuned to E, C and then G respectively. The standard way of tuning a ukulele to GCEA is to have the G on that string that is nearest the ceiling actually a higher G in pitch than the next string (the C-string or third string). With a lot of standard stringed instruments, particularly the guitar, as you pluck from the string nearest the ceiling down through the strings to the one nearest the floor, the notes get higher in relation to each other. On a standard tuned uke, that string nearest the ceiling is actually higher than both of the next two strings and its pitch sits between the E and the A strings. If you imagine the keys on a piano keyboard, you will probably know that the notes from A through to C repeat up the keyboard over and over. By tuning with a high G on a ukulele, the G-string is not tuned to the G below C, but the G _above_ C. This gives the ukulele its bright uke like sound and is the traditional tuning method. If you have a soprano uke you will note that your G-string is thinner, not thicker than the C-string, and this is because it is designed to be tuned higher. It creates a ringing chiming treble sound to the strum that, well, that makes the ukulele sound like a ukulele! It is possible, however, to tune the instrument with a G that is lower than the C-string and that is called Low G tuning.

Low G tuning means tuning the string nearest the ceiling (the fourth string) to the G that is one whole octave below the high G on a standard tuned ukulele. Whilst you are still playing the same notes (GCEA) this cuts out the brighter G and makes the ukulele sound a little more mellow by adding more bass to the sound. Some also suggest it makes the larger ukulele sizes sound more "guitar like" and I would agree with that. To do this, I would not however advise using your standard high G strings, as that thin G-string will end up too slack for such a low tuning. To do so, you need to ideally purchase some low G-strings, which have a thicker G-string, or find a single low G which are available in some stores. The string is otherwise identical to other uke strings but will be thicker than a high G-string, and in some cases you can get what is called a "wound" G-string. This is a normal string wrapped in a thin coil of steel wire much as you will find on an acoustic guitar. A wound string accentuates that low G even more and gives you more of a bass sound to your playing although some players suggest they can create something of a bass overkill on the instrument so do be careful.

I would suggest that if you are wishing to try out playing in Low G, you should really only do so on a concert or tenor uke, as the soprano is really designed for that traditional high G sound. Some people do try a low G on a soprano, but it is not to my personal taste.

Whether you choose to try playing with a Low G is purely personal choice. I personally think the low G makes the uke sound too much like a guitar, and prefer the high G sound on all my instruments including the tenor scale ukes. That said, I can think of some songs where that extra bass of a low G would really add to the strum, so, never say never!

As a final couple of points regarding Low G, bear in mind that if you are installing a heavy wound low G string, you may well need to widen your nut slot for that string, and that isn't something that is easily reversed. Some ukes, such as Mainland ukuleles, come with a removable nut designed for people who want to switch tunings (i.e. you prepare two nuts and swap them when needed) but you may find on a lot of other instruments that the nut is fairly firmly glued in place. Also, if you tune your ukulele using a standard pitch pipe as opposed to a clip on tuner, you may struggle using it to tune the Low G, as it will be made to work best with a high G.

But let's now move back to the standard, high G tuning, and its name, which is 'Re-entrant Tuning'. Re-entrant tuning on a stringed instrument really just means that the strings don't run from low to high (or high to low) in pitch as you move through the strings. This is something found on a range of stringed instruments, including the lute, the five string banjo, and traditionally tuned ukuleles. In the world of uke, soprano ukuleles are traditionally tuned re-entrant, and most people play concerts and some tenors this way. Where you have a ukulele tuned in re-entrant tuning, it will be referred to as having a high G or a high 4th.

As we discussed above, the G-string on a standard tuned ukulele is higher than the next two strings, and as such the notes plucked on the strings from one through to four don't descend in pitch. This break in the descending notes is called the 're-entry'. Very NASA don't you think..?

Where a lot of people get confused is they think this high string is a completely different note when it actually isn't. A G note is a G note, but what we have on a high G is a G an octave above the G that would have been played if the notes were allowed to continue to descend deeper. As such, finger positions for chord shapes and finger picking doesn't need to change when switching between high or low G, because it is still a G.

So, if it is still a G, what is the point? Well, on the ukulele, quite simply it brings that bit of extra chime and sparkle to your strumming that would not be there with a deeper G note. This gives the uke what I think is its trademark sound.

That's it really - not very complicated, but useful to know. If you have a soprano ukulele, as I say above I really think they are best tuned to high G (re-entrant), but when you get into Concerts and especially Tenors, you can think about a low G. Just remember to buy those strings labeled as Low G!

35. BASIC THEORY PT2 – MAJOR CHORDS

Time to look again at some basic music theory for the ukulele. In this short chapter we will be looking at the Major chords.

Firstly, what exactly is a chord? Put simply, a chord is just a collection of notes played together. In fact any series of notes combining two, three or four notes on a ukulele is technically a chord. The most common of these are those that sound most pleasing and work well within musical structure, and you will see most of the most common on any ukulele chord chart such as those available on the Got A Ukulele website. Many people simply take a chord chart and learn to memorise the shapes without giving much more thought as to what is actually happening within the music, but perhaps you want to know a little more than that.

In this chapter we will just be dealing with Major Chords - these are the chords that are represented by a single letter such as C, D, F and G, without any small m, 7 or other descriptions after them (we will deal with those in another chapter).

A chord name is always representative of the first or root note that is played in the collection of notes. As such in an A chord, the root note in the chord is an A, and in a C chord, the root note is a C. Simple enough!

To make up the chord, we take that first root note and then add what is called the third and the fifth in the major scale of that root note. These three notes become the triad, being the root, the third and the fifth interval In the first theory chapter of this book we explained how the notes progressed over the strings of the ukulele, and that each note was a semitone apart. To understand how chords work you need to know that the third of the root that we are looking for is four semitones above the root note, and the fifth of the root note is seven semitones above.

So taking the C Major chord, we start with our root note of C. The third of the root is the note four semitones above the C. If we remember how the notes progress, the progression of notes four semitones above C would run as follows

1 – C# / Db

2 – D

3 – D# / Eb

4 - E

Therefore our next note, four semitones up is an E.

To get the next note of the C chord, we continue the sequence up to seven semitones from C, and if you follow the same scale of notes you will find that takes us to a G note.

Using this theory of root, third and fifth, we now know that the notes in a C chord are C, E and G.

Now, there are four strings on the ukulele, tuned G, C, E and A. To form the chord we need to ensure that we are picking out the notes C, E and G. when strummed. Helpfully with the C chord, three of the strings on the ukulele are naturally tuned to G, C and E when played open (the three nearest the ceiling!). We can therefore play those open and know that they will work well with the C chord. Our problem string is the first string, the one nearest the floor. If we were to play that open in the chord we would get an A, and that wouldn't work, in fact it would create a whole different chord. If, however, we fret that string at the third fret, we know from our notes theory that we get another C note. By doing that you are fingering the simplest form of the C chord made up of the notes G, C, E and C.

Let's try that again with the A chord. Our root note for the A chord is, of course A. The third of the root is four semitones above an A which is C# and the fifth of the root (seven semitones) is an E. We therefore need to look at the ukulele and ensure that when strummed we are only playing the notes A, C# and E.

Our first string nearest the floor plays an A when strummed open so we can leave that alone. The second string plays an E when open, so we can leave that one alone also. Our third string played open is a C which would be incorrect in an A chord, so by fretting that at the first fret we know we get our required C#. Our fourth string plays a G when open which is no good for an A chord either, but be fretting up two frets we get an A note which is one of our required notes in the chord. Playing these frets gives you an A using the notes A, C#, E and A.

Using this theory you can work out the fingerings for all of the major chords. Usually, the simplest form of the chord is to find the easiest fingerings that create the desired notes nearest to the nut, but you can play all of the major chords in a variety of ways all over the neck, so long as the notes you are playing fit with the three notes of the chord, the root, the third of the root and the fifth.

Have a look at the chord chart on Got A Ukulele, picking out the major chords and use this theory to check how this works with the others.

36. UKULELE FINISHES

So you have decided to take the plunge into the world of ukulele, and perhaps you are playing a fairly basic plain model at the moment. You decide to upgrade and you may find yourself bewildered by the range that is out there. You may also find yourself wondering about the different finishes that are available on the ukulele, and do they affect the instrument in any way?

The "finish" of the ukulele is the way the wood on the top, back and sides is treated before the instrument is finally complete. In the main, the finish is usually just cosmetic, but the debate on whether it affects the actual sound of the instrument is something that rages on many discussion forums between uke players. Listed below are the main types of ukulele finish you will come across.

GLOSS

A gloss finish, as it's name suggests, leaves a very shiny, almost mirror like finish on the ukulele. It is usually created with the application of a type of varnish such as nitrocellulose, polyurethane or similar and polished to a high shine finish with several layers that are separately worked back with increasingly fine grades of a sanding material. A gloss finish can really bring out the "shimmer" in some nicer wood grains, reflects light and can make an instrument look very classy.

A good quality glossy finish could well make the ukulele more expensive as it naturally takes more time in the building to get the mirror like shine. In that respect, there are many cheap ukes on the market with less then high quality gloss finishes achieved by applying the gloss varnish in thick gloopy coats. This is something I would, personally, avoid. Tell tale signs of such a poor finish are drips or "pooling" of the excess varnish around the sound hole, and at the heel of the neck where it joins the body. I have seen some instruments where dried varnish has actually formed a hard drip shape hanging inside the instrument off the edge of the sound hole. A good quality gloss finish should be not thicker than it needs to be, and there should be no signs of too much being applied anywhere on the instrument.

A gloss finish will also serve to protect the underlying wood of the instrument more than a matte finish as discussed below, but conversely they are more prone to highlighting scratches and chips. Gloss finishes also create something of a fingerprint magnet – prepare for lots of polishing to keep your uke looking tip top!

SATIN / MATTE

A satin or matte finish absorbs more light than it reflects giving it a dull and unshiny look. When I describe that in words it sounds horrible, but it actually looks very natural and allows the wood to show itself off on its own. Whilst I say above that the gloss finish looks classy, many players prefer the understated class that a matte finish brings to an instrument. Heck, the ukulele is made of wood, so why not let the wood celebrate itself and show off? Such finishes may be created using very thin applications of the same lacquers used for gloss, but without polishing, or perhaps with a very thin rubbing varnish, lightly applied and left to dry. They can also be created using an application of a wood oil or wax.

When commercial ukuleles first appeared in the early 1900's, this was the only finish available and as such, many traditionalists suggest this is the better finish for the instrument.

The downside to the coating being so thin on a matte finish means that any knocks and dings you give your instrument are more likely to scratch or dent the actual wood underneath. Matte finishes also tend to show fingernail scratches from strumming, and can generate shiny patches where the arm has been holding the instrument.

PAINTED UKES

Painted finishes, using a variety of bright and bold colours is usually the preserve of the cheaper ukulele market, and on novelty ukuleles. I have nothing against these, but again, as is the case with gloss, a heavily applied paint finish can look particularly cheap and messy.

That said, paint, when professionally applied can

appear on higher end instruments and look very impressive indeed. Bruko, the German handmade manufacturer make some ukes with a fine spray painted finish, and most of the tops on Fleas and Fluke ukuleles are painted. Both of those manufacturers make excellent, professional quality instruments and choose to use the paint route to create a more unique looking instrument.

DOES IT MAKE A DIFFERENCE?

As I said in the introduction to this chapter, I am of the view that finish is, in the main, a cosmetic factor only. There is much written about whether a gloss finish and a satin finish differ in sound.

This debate comes about because of the potential for impact on the vibrating parts of the ukulele, as those parts are what give the instrument its tone. Anything that is "added" to the soundboard, the part of the uke that vibrates to amplify the sound can, theoretically, affect its efficiency to do so or at least change it in some way. If two completely identical instruments were played side by side, with identical set up and strings, it may be expected that a satin finish will allow for a louder sound, and a gloss finish a very slightly softer sound. Whether it changes the tone of the instrument though is, in my view, entirely subjective and I try not to get drawn into such arguments. Even with the same setup and strings, no two instruments or pieces of wood are identical and as such I find the comparison a hard one to make.

Worse still are the arguments that rage comparing matte and gloss finishes on completely different ukes - this to me seems a nonsense as a large number of other factors need to come in to play (even before you take on board the fact that the sound is subjective anyway). How the instrument is made, braced, how big the sound hole is, the type of strings, the type of player, solid or laminated wood, type of wood all have a far greater impact on sound than whether one is gloss or matte.

My advice is to choose your instrument based on its quality, how it plays and how it looks and sounds to you. If you are settled on one of two instruments that are otherwise sound and feel just right for you, your choice on gloss or matte should be made based on which you prefer the look of. There is no right or wrong, and I play both!

37. WHATS IN MY GIG BAG?

If you have bought a ukulele, then hopefully you have fallen in love with it. If that has happened, you will find that you want to take your ukulele with you everywhere - to work, on holiday, to the shops (!). It's a portable instrument so why not? You may also be thinking about gigging or busking with your instrument, which is great news.

If that is the case, then what should you consider taking with you when you go out and about with your instrument? What is the essential gear list that no ukulele player should be without if they want to be prepared? I will therefore share with you the items that always go with my uke if I am gigging, busking, jamming, or taking it away from home for extended periods.

Case - Kind of obvious, but if you are travelling anywhere with a ukulele, or taking it to gigs you REALLY SHOULD invest in a good case. I discussed cases in an earlier chapter, but generally, how much you spend depends on how important the ukulele is to you. You may be happy with a soft cloth or padded zippered case, which will be fine for preventing knocks and scratches. A hard case will, however provide more protection from being crushed or dropped and is really essential if travelling where the ukulele is being stowed.

Spare strings - Even if I have just put a new set on the ukulele before I leave the house, I always keep a spare set of strings in my case. You never know when you might get a break, and even those new strings could run into trouble. They don't cost a great deal and the peace of mind having a set in a case is worth it. I've also used spare strings to give to other players I am strumming with when they have suffered a break – us uke players are a friendly bunch!

Tuner - I carry two tuners at all times. I carry a clip on tuner (I use a model made by Snark), which is the method I use for 99% of my tuning. I also carry a cheap pitchpipe tuner in my case for the unlikely eventuality my clip on tuner breaks or the more likely chance that the battery dies. Again, when playing with others, expect your tuner to help others out as well as you!

Small screwdriver - for tightening friction tuning pegs.

Soft polishing cloth - I always carry a soft cloth and get myself in the habit of wiping down the instrument, particularly the neck after a session. It's not that I have some obsession with cleanliness, but cleaning the strings of the grease, grime and beer that naturally accumulates when playing in a pub will serve to help lengthen their life.

Strap – I rarely use a ukulele strap but for busking when standing up it can be a great help to stop the instrument from slipping. I personally use a strap called a Uke Leash, which is a genius bit of design and takes up virtually no space in my ukulele case. Would urge you check them out online – speak to

Lori!

Songbook - I print my ukulele lyrics and chords on to A4 sheets of paper and keep them inside clear plastic wallets bound in a 4 ring binder. The plastic wallets stop them getting dog-eared or drenched by spilled beer or the rain if I am outdoors! The added benefit to using the wallets is that it makes it very easy to swap song sheets in and out to suit a session or my tastes at the time. I also keep an extensive ukulele chord chart in the back of the binder in case an obscure chord I haven't committed to memory challenges me. The chord chart is always useful for helping other players out too.

Hat – well, ok, not always, but for busking, certainly. Something to pass around to collect the pennies!

Enthusiasm and a sense of humour – but of course!

It's not a lot to take along - the uke is a simple and portable instrument and you don't want to be bogged down with too much gear. The above should, however, ensure you never get into a tight spot!

38. JAMMING, BUSKING AND PERFORMING

So you have bought your first ukulele, and you are (but of course!) having huge amounts of fun with it. Then the time finally comes, you get asked to go and play with others. Playing in public? To an audience? Of real people?? I couldn't possibly! Could I?

The fact is though, that once you are over the initial hump of getting used to playing some basic chords and strums, the singular best way to improve your playing and your confidence is to play with or for other people. A reception to the music you make really is the best way you can judge your abilities and improve on them. Now, before I send you into a complete panic attack, I'm not suggesting you should be booking yourself in for a residency at Caesars Palace (that comes later...). There are, though, many options available to you that I would urge you to try as you progress

MAKE A VIDEO RECORDING

Not everybody lives in an area with easy access to lots of other people who play the ukulele, and it may be that you are just not able to get out and about to perform in public for a variety of reasons. This is where the video, and by that I mean uploading a recording of yourself to something like YouTube or a Ukulele site, is a superb and easy way of getting quick feedback on your performances. Not only can others look at your work, but the very act of watching and listening to yourself in a recording is a sure fire way to improving your skills. The first time you do it you may find it impossible and unbearable to listen to yourself – that is perfectly normal. You may dislike your voice, your playing or even both, but this is where you can spot the mistakes you are making. Have faith in yourself though and give it a try. If you don't like the results then it's only you who has to see it. That said, I would urge you not to delete anything as nothing will give you a boost in support more than going back in a years time to see just how far you have come! In terms of equipment, most mobile phones these days are capable of recording decent quality video so you don't need a setup worthy of Steven Spielberg. That said, any video camera that you can easily load onto a PC works fine. I use a device called a Creative Vado, or I use my Mac webcam.

You can then give some serious thought to putting a video or two up on the public internet for other people to see, in fact for the whole world to see (gulp!). There is a small chance that may get some nasty words from a few (hurr hurr that's a toy guitar...), but ignore them, as on the whole you will most likely find really helpful constructive criticism. The Ukulele Underground Forum is a great place to alert people to your videos and seek feedback – just share the link to the YouTube page (or wherever you have the video hosted) and ask people for honest feedback. Listen to your reviewers and take on board the tips they give you to improve your work. Top tip – don't argue with your reviewers, it really isn't worth it! Perhaps the most famous success story of performing in this way is the wonderful ukulele artist Julia Nunes who started out performing on YouTube and is now a gigging and recording musician who has played live with the likes of Ben Folds. My good pal Rae Carter may well be heading in the same direction and if you read the Got A Ukulele site you may have seen some of his videos. He's had tens of thousands of video views, is regularly gigging and recently had an EP recorded which is available on the iTunes store. You never know, that could be you!

RECORD A TRACK

Home audio recording is now becoming easier and easier, and with very little equipment you can easily record a track in your bedroom if you wish. The Audioboo website is a great resource for putting up a recording direct from your computer with no need for any other equipment (heck, you can do it from your mobile phone!), but you could go the whole hog and get a good microphone and recording set up to create a properly mixed track on your computer and upload that to the web. Whether you want to simply put a track out for free is up to you, but iTunes now make it possible for anybody to put a song on their service and make it available to be sold – quite a change in the music business!

Like recording video, recording audio of yourself

singing and playing is a superb practice tool, as you will easily spot your weak points and mistakes. Just make sure you try to learn from them!

TRY JAMMING

How does Bob Marley like his dougnuts? Wi' Jammin'. Sorry, silly joke couldn't resist.

Jamming is the term given to a no rules, no planning strum with other like-minded people for the sheer fun of it.

Playing with other ukulele players is a brilliant way to improve your skills and confidence, and being a group activity you are sure to help each other out, or give each other ideas as to new songs to practice so everybody gains, thus, driving you on. You can do this as informally as you like, perhaps just with friends in your living room or garden, or perhaps ask at your local pub or club if they would mind you playing in their premises, thereby potentially enticing others to join in and build a bigger group. I regularly play this way with friends and it is a huge amount of fun. We play in a local pub an on occasion have ended up with quite an audience singing along with us!

The joy of having a ukulele jam is that there are no real rules, and you are playing for fun. You can try to take centre stage if you like, but equally, you may be happier just strumming in the background. It will depend on your confidence and your mood on the particular occasion, but I guarantee that doing this regularly will have see your playing take off. Be sensitive to the tastes of others and try not to dominate a session by insisting everybody play your songs, let everyone take a turn and join in with other songs as this way you will naturally add to your song list.

If you want to jam a little more formally there are a huge range of clubs and societies out there who will welcome you with open arms and there is a huge (and growing) list of ukulele clubs and groups around the world on the Got A Ukulele website. Who knows, playing with a club informally this way could get you noticed, as has happened with some ukulele friends of mine who run a club called UkeJam in Godalming, UK. They haven't been playing as a club for all that long (only just over a year), but during 2011 they were asked to play a set on the acoustic stage of the Guildford Festival and played a support slot for a Hayseed Dixie show in the UK. A real success story. The beauty of getting involved in a club (aside from making new friends!) is that there may well be a little more structure to the playing. It is likely the organisers will provide guidance and song sheets for you to play, and you will be dropping in to a group who already has something of a set list to work with.

BE A BUSKER

Perhaps this is one for when you are little more seasoned with your playing and have a few good songs under your belt, but this form of playing, in the town centre or park near to you is both a daunting and extremely rewarding experience. You can do this with friends or solo, but having done this myself can vouch for the fact that the more "unusual" aspect that the ukulele carries (than say, the guitar) will likely draw more people to watch you. It can, of course, be extremely nerve-wracking, and on a cold wet day, depressing too. The plus side, of course, is that if you are good you could go home at the end of the day with some of money in your pocket! Please, please though, check first with your local bye-laws as to whether you need a licence to busk in your area unless you want a tap on the shoulder from the authorities!

If you are able to busk, think carefully about the location. There is little point setting up next to something noisy (and certainly not next to another busker – that is terribly bad form that could get you a few stares or a possible whack on the nose with the business end of the adjacent guitar player!), and equally no point setting up where there are no people. Town squares are the obvious place to consider, and if permitted, stations, metros, subways and the like. If you are playing outside a shop you might want to also ask permission of the storeowner beforehand. Either way, engage with the public, smile, play contemporary songs for all ages, and most of all, have fun.

OPEN MIC SPOTS

Open Mics are events, usually put on at local pubs, bars or clubs, where anyone can turn up and book a slot to take to the stage and perform a song or two in front of an audience for the sheer fun of it. You are very unlikely to get paid (though you may get a free drink), and you may not even get listened to, but this is a real step into professional performing where you have to stand on your own two feet and get your style and sound out there to the general public. Bear in mind, with a small instrument like a ukulele that you almost certainly will need to consider some form of amplification both for your instrument and your voice if you don't want to get lost in the hubbub of the audience.

The step up from a jam session or busking to an open mic performance is considerable. The key difference is that, in the first two examples, you are playing and an audience might or might not gather, and as such there is much less pressure. At an open mic, you may be introduced to the stage to stand in front of an audience who turned up specifically to watch the acts. As such they are EXPECTING to be entertained and may well show their displeasure if you let them down!

GIGS

Gigs? Really? That's a bit advanced, I hear you cry. Well, not really and if you have had some fun busking or in an open mic session this really is the next step. I am talking about local circuits that don't require much planning other than finding out which pubs and clubs have regular local music spots and asking to have a turn. A gig expands on an open mic as the proprietor as well as the audience will be expecting you to fill a night with songs – lots of songs so make sure you have plenty to hand. There is usually no issue with having your music and lyrics on a stand in front of you if you are good enough, but even better to play unaided. As with open mics, you really need to prepare to be electrified unless you are gigging with many of you when the combined sound will do the trick. Make sure you understand in advance what the venue owner will and wont be providing to make sure you don't get caught short, and don't forget your tuner, spare strings and a lot of bottle. You may be lucky enough to get a token payment, and you may get paid in drinks. Note – save the drinks for another night. A drunken ukulele player on stage is not a happy site – trust me I know....(not me you understand!). Make a mark with some small gigs and expect to be asked to come back or perhaps play bigger venues.

Beyond that, the sky really is the limit. If you really don't like the idea of playing in public, I'd still urge you to try to play with good friends or at least record yourself and listen to it back. It's without a doubt one of the best ways to progress your playing. Whatever you choose, you are going to be nervous and unsure when you first give it a try, but that will pass with more experience, and with more experience comes better playing and more fun. It's all good! Get out there and play!

39. MUSICAL BARRIERS

Learning anything, whether it is a musical instrument or not requires dedication, effort and resolve. In learning a new skill you will always hit 'barriers' where you feel like you want to give up, that it's never going to work and that you have made a mistake in choosing to take this on. This happens to many people when learning the ukulele, and it's nothing to be scared of.

I repeatedly point out to beginners that the ukulele is an easy instrument to start to learn and I stand by that. In my opinion it has one of the shallowest learning curves of any instrument meaning most beginners can get something meaningful out of it in weeks, days, or even hours and minutes. But, it takes a considerable period to become proficient, to master the instrument at hand, and unless you are a total natural, you will hit walls that you will think are impossible to break through. The trick is to stay dedicated and work through them. Break down your musical barriers!

The first barrier many people hit, particularly if they

have never played strings before are the sore fingertips or aching fingers and hands. This is extremely common and something that only eases with more playing, as you need to build up harder skin in the form of callouses to overcome the pain. I am not trying to be dismissive but it really is that simple. It will, however, be short lived and improve with more playing. Go back to the chapter on sore fingers for more advice on this.

Another cause of pain you may encounter will be aches and cramps. Again, this is perfectly normal. You are asking your fingers to move and stretch into unnatural positions and your muscles and tendons need to learn the shapes you are creating. In these cases, if you are in pain, don't play on regardless or you may cause some more serious damage. Take a break! Sure, only continued practice will stop the pain occurring, but you need to listen to your body's signals and know when to ease up. You should also consider finger-stretching exercises as described earlier, but also easily found in video guides on the Internet.

Moving on to the other hand, the next most common barrier is getting comfortable with strumming. For many, it is a real struggle to get your playing flowing naturally and sounding professional. In my opinion the biggest mistake many make is to try to learn something far to complex before mastering more basic songs and patterns. Keep it simple when you are starting out - if you enjoy your uke you will be playing it for many more years. You have all the time in the world to learn that favourite song with 15 chords and a tempo of 100 miles per hour! The first strum you need to master is just some basic up and down in a steady rhythm, and the ability to keep it steady throughout the length of a song. Consider investing in a metronome if you struggle to keep time, and again, playing with others is a huge help in this area as you have a natural group of pace setters sat with you. It may sound boring but if you don't master a basic rhythm, you will always struggle. What is that old saying? Don't try running before you can walk.

And putting all this together, you will then continue to hit barriers, even when you become an accomplished player. You may find you have issues playing with other people, in public, in singing along with the ukulele, and it is all perfectly normal and part of learning a new skill. I still hit new barriers when trying a particularly complex strum, or chord change, or just songs and patterns that are new to me. The answer, as with even the most basic barriers is to keep at it. If it's not working for you, take a break and play something else, try another technique and come back to it another day. You are not alone though, and around the world thousands of new players are hitting the same stumbling blocks all the time. A beginner turns into a player for life when they learn to break through the rough spots.

I hope this inspires and supports new players who are reading. You are not alone, and we all go through what you are going through, just keep pressing on and before you know it, you'll be playing freely and advising other new players how to break their own barriers!

Good luck as always, and enjoy it!

40. BASIC THEORY PT3 – MINOR CHORDS

In the earlier chapter of this book we looked at Major ukulele chords and how they are formed from the root, the third of the root and the fifth of the root notes in the scale. It is important for any player that you know the major chords, but you will not get very far without some variations on those. In this chapter we move on to look at Minor Chords.

A minor chord is a variation on the major chords we looked at earlier, and is shown in chord notation with a small "m" symbol after the note of the chord name, like Am, Cm and so on. The minor chords are often referred to as the 'sad' chords in music, and provide real expression to you songs. Don't let that get you down – sad can also create uplifting music and you will be surprised just how many songs really do turn on the minor chords and scales.

As I said above, when we looked at the major chords we saw that a major chord is made up of the first, third and fifth of the scale of the chord you are playing in.

A minor chord is exactly the same, but the third of the root note is played down one half a tone (or flat).

Using our example from the chapter on major chords, and looking back at the A chord, we learned that the A was made up of the notes A, C# and E. For the Am chord, we need to take that middle note, (the third of the root), down a half tone to flatten it. Taking a C# down a step (half a tone) takes it to a C note. We therefore know that for Am, we need the notes A, C and E on the Uke.

Looking at the notes on the fingerboard, the A note remains the same as in the Major A chord, i.e. the G string at the second fret. Unlike the A major chord though, for the Am, the next note is not a C# but a C. We know that the third string on a uke is a C when played open, so now it doesn't need fretting unlike in the major version of the chord. The first and second strings also can be left alone because they play A and E respectively as in the A major, so work for this chord also.

And that's it! To turn any major chord into a minor, just take that third, middle note in your chord down a half tone. Easy - try it with the other major chords you learned.

Good luck!

41. MOVING FROM GUITAR TO UKULELE

Whilst the ukulele is an accessible instrument for those with no musical background whatsoever, it does also seem to attract those who have played the big brother instrument, the guitar, before. I thought therefore I would explain the links between the two instruments, and give you my take on why the uke is a great choice for any guitar player to consider.

I actually read in and online discussion recently that somebody stated that the ukulele was the instrument people chose to learn because they 'couldn't be bothered to learn the guitar'. That annoyed me, not least because this particular ukulele player started out playing guitar (and still does!) but because of how wrong a statement it is. The statement suggests that the ukulele is easier than the guitar when really; to truly master the uke requires similar levels of commitment and skill. Anyone who thinks playing a ukulele is easy should simply check out any video of Jake Shimabukuro or James Hill! But the statement is also erroneous because there are a huge number of celebrity players out there who play both uke and guitar and take pleasure from both. Paul McCartney and the late George Harrison are obvious examples, but Elvis Costello, Bruce Springsteen, Pete Townshend are amongst many others who get pleasure from the uke despite being more commonly associated with the guitar. Besides all that, and instrument is an instrument and no one thing is better than any other.

So, I write this as somebody who, before picking up the ukulele a few years ago, had played guitar (both acoustic and electric) for some twenty years previously. That certainly made my learning of the ukulele much quicker, and other friends I know who play guitar and have made the transition say the same thing. But why is that?

Before I give you my views, I should make it clear that this is not intended to be a snub to the guitar community. The ukulele is not a replacement for a guitar; it's a complimentary instrument. In fact, it's just another instrument full stop and the world is a big place that can fit both! I still adore playing the guitar, and in many ways the guitar can provide options that are just not there with a uke. That said, the uke has many attractions to a guitar player, and if you are a player of six strings reading this, perhaps this may give you the push to try the ukulele.

EASE OF TRANSITION

Standard ukulele tuning shares much with the standard six string guitar tuning. In fact the standard GCEA tuning of a ukulele plays exactly the same as the DGBE (first four strings) of a guitar as if you had a capo across the fifth fret. As such, the relationship between the notes on the strings is identical, and the chord shapes will be familiar to any guitarist. If you fret a D shape on the guitar, that shape works on the ukulele too, but because of the higher tuning, plays you a G chord. If you fret a guitar G chord shape on the uke, you only need one finger as the E and A equivalent guitar strings are not there on the ukulele. As such, you just hold the first string at the third fret, and you get a C chord. This ease of transition makes picking up a uke very straightforward for anyone who understands the guitar.

It's not just about music theory though. A common complaint for many new ukers is sore fingertips and aching fingers from stretching and playing such awkward shapes. If you have played a guitar for long enough you simply won't have to deal with that and you will find the uke very easy on the fingertips. There is, however, one common gripe for a guitar player approaching the ukulele for the first time, and that is the much smaller fretting area on the neck. A guitar is, naturally, much wider, and when moving to a ukulele many guitar players struggle at first to get those fingers previously accustomed to space cramped together! For this reason, many guitar players who move to ukulele choose to start out with a concert or a tenor scale instrument as it provides a little more room for the fingertips. Strumming, holding and general technique honed on a guitar will also translate to the ukulele easily as the principles are the same.

PORTABILITY AND PRICE

Sure, many guitarists carry their instruments with

them wherever they go. It is a fact though that many guitarists do go on the hunt for portable travel guitars that they can more easily carry when trekking, camping, going on holiday etc. Why go for a travel guitar when you can go with a ukulele - the ultimate in musical portability? Have you ever tried getting a full sized guitar through an airport in hand luggage? Not problem with a soprano ukulele - heck, you could probably get away with taking two! (a homage to George Harrison who allegedly always travelled with several ukuleles so that he didn't have to play on his own!)

The thing about the ukulele size is that it REALLY can go anywhere with you. I leave one in my car, take one with me on business trips, and can easily sling one over my shoulder on walks to the park. There is really no excuse to not have a ukulele with you wherever you are, and that in turn leads to it being played more frequently. Got five minutes to spare? Have a strum! (I obviously urge common sense here and would suggest starting strumming in a library, church christening or cinema may all equally be considered bad form..!)

Do you have limited space in your living room?

Can't stand a guitar up in it? No problem with a ukulele - I keep one tucked by the side of my sofa - you wouldn't even know it was there, but it's always available for me to pick it up and play it in seconds. Actually, what am I saying, I have several tucked down the side of the sofa, and in other rooms in the house too, but I am coming to terms with my problem..

Price is also a factor. Whilst both guitars and ukes have their bargain basement and premium ends to the price scales, it is a fact that you can get a lot of useable ukulele for a lot less than you would spend on a cheaper guitar. The Makala Dolphin for example, whilst not a "pro" instrument by any means has a great sound, is tough as old boots, and retails for a measly £30 in the UK. I dread to think what the quality would be of a guitar for £30.

FOR QUIET TIMES

Have you ever been in a situation with a guitar where you cannot play it because you are going to disturb someone else? Whilst a ukulele still makes its own noise, it is much easier to play a uke at very soft and low volume than it is with a guitar, whilst still producing worthwhile tone. It's the late night instrument!

THE FUN AND SOCIAL FACTORS

Let's face it, guitars are everywhere and have been for a long time, but the ukulele holds that "something different" tag. Buskers on most street corners have guitars, and music spots in local clubs and bars often feature the same. A ukulele however, stands out! Speaking as somebody who has played both guitar and ukulele in public jam sessions and busking, I can honestly say that the humble uke sparks up more interest, generates more questions, and puts more smiles on faces than a guitar ever did! (no jokes about my guitar playing please..) I have never seen somebody walk into a bar or pub where a jam session is taking place and say, "ooh look, that's a guitar!". When I play uke in public I can guarantee that every night somebody will come over and ask what it is, or point out, "is that a ukulele? I've always fancied playing one of those", and then stay around to have a listen. It's the interesting instrument!

The more timid, less overpowering sound of a ukulele also makes it the perfect instrument to play in large groups of people without getting the police called around for disturbing the peace. My friends and I have played to a crowded pub full of people with half a dozen ukuleles strummed at full throttle without it taking over the place for other people. That's not something we could sensibly do with six guitars. Volume aside, we couldn't fit them all around the table!

So those are my thoughts. As I say, the ukulele doesn't replace the guitar, and the guitar has its own benefits that the uke cannot compete with (range of tones and voices being the obvious), but this guitar / ukulele player thinks that anyone who has fun with six strings should certainly try their hand with four! Oh, and of course, when you start to improve with the ukulele it obviously stands you in very good stead to moving on to the guitar, but this is a ukulele book so don't tell anyone I said that..

42. STARTING A UKULELE CLUB

If you are a reader of Got A Ukulele, you will have noticed that I do sing the praises of ukulele clubs and societies as being great places for the beginner to learn and build confidence. You will have read that in this very book too but I do bang on about it for a reason! I do hope that you have a look at the club listing on Got A Ukulele and try to get along to one, but what if there is no club near you? Could you start one up? Why not!

Starting a ukulele club isn't actually as tough as you may think it would be. In fact it's just an informal gathering of like-minded people who want to change the world with four strings whilst keeping smiles on their faces. When you break it down it is really just about venue, promotion and organisation. So, what can I advise?

THE VENUE AND TIMING

Choosing the right venue for a club meeting place is extremely important. You need to think about numbers, noise, whether you do or you don't want an audience and how easy it would be for potential new members to attend on a regular basis.

I think the ukulele is booming, but unless you are expecting an enormous growth in membership overnight, you are not going to need the Royal Albert Hall on standby. Bear in mind however that, as a club grows you may also regret choosing the six-foot square back room of the local bar with four chairs and a single light bulb.

The most obvious venues are pubs, bars, clubs and village halls. Whichever you choose, think of somewhere easily accessible and you must of course get permission beforehand. You may find some venues want to charge for the privilege, but conversely you may find that many, pubs in particular may welcome the trade and offer you a room or a corner for nothing on the basis it brings more customers through the door. Explain that you are not intending to make huge amounts of noise (ukes are acoustic!). Recently we had to move our regular ukulele jam to a different venue for a single night. We asked the staff if we could play and they looked in horror when we said there were about six of us, obviously expecting a huge racket. A quick strum of the ukulele for the proprietor showed her that the sound was really rather sweet and unobtrusive. She smiled and said of course we could play!

In terms of the attributes the room needs to provide, unless you are going to provide lots of sheet music stands at your own expense, you need a room with enough seats, but more importantly large tables for people to lay out song sheets, tuners and cases, without anyone feeling out on a limb and unable to join in. This may require some table re-arranging before the club meets, but it will be far better for everyone to see, and importantly, hear everyone else. Beginner ukulele players benefit massively from being able to watch the finger positions of other players, but someone stuck with their back to the rest of the club in a corner will just not hear the sound well enough to play along very well.

Also, think about the most appropriate day to suggest to the venue owner (and time). In the case of a pub or a bar you would be silly to expect to get the front room reserved at eight on a Friday night.

For this reason, most clubs tend to meet midweek in the evening or perhaps on a quiet afternoon at a weekend. Frequency is an issue to discuss with future members to sound out what they think seems right. Some clubs meet weekly, but more frequently people seem to meet every other week or once a month allowing members time to practice between sessions. Many clubs allow members to perform their own solo spots, or examples of work they have been practicing at home.

PROMOTING THE CLUB

I write this section on the basis that you are not looking to pay for advertising. If you have just landed a fortune from the will of your Great Great uncle Eric (rest in peace Eric), then be my guest, but most will want to promote their club for little or money. (note- some clubs do charge membership subs to allow for costs such as photocopying, but that is something you need to work out with members to ensure monies are transparent and nobody brings your treasurer role into question!)

The most obvious place to advertise is the venue

itself. Ask if you can put up some flyers with details of the event in the pub or club, particularly in the windows. You could go further and put some flyers up on lampposts in your town if permitted (but remember, Bill Stickers will be prosecuted....) or hand them out around town. Keep them fresh and replace any tatty ones promptly and get your friends to spread the word too. I'd avoid putting cards in telephone boxes unless you want to attract a different sort of clientele altogether..

Scout the local newspapers, particularly free ones as some do offer free listings in their entertainment and classifieds sections on occasion. If you can get a free listing, use it!

Beyond that, the Internet is your friend. There are multitudes of ways you can spread the word about your new club, but those I'd recommend as being the most helpful are Facebook, Twitter, Google Plus and a Blog. On Facebook and Google, start by using your own timeline as a means to announce the club, and ask your friends to share your posts. As well as mentioning the club on your own timeline, make sure you post it in the various ukulele groups that exist on the site (just do a search for groups with the word 'ukulele'). Also check out groups that are specific to your location and do the same. At the same time set up both a Facebook page for your club which holds all the details for new members including locations and times, and a new private group to add members to and promote both in the same way (but don't spam!). The more links you have flying around, the better as Social Networking thrives on your messages being shared and then re-shared. As your members grow, you can add them to your Facebook Group and share songs and ideas with the membership directly. On Twitter, make your announcement using the hashtag #ukulele and also a hashtag for your town such as #Warwick or #Idaho. (A hashtag is the act of putting the # symbol directly in front of a single phrase with no spaces, that allows those tweets to be grouped together when people search). People who use Twitter regularly search those tags and you may get a bite, and better still a Re-Tweet to other people. A Blog is much more hard work to build an audience, but it would be good for your club to at least have a homepage with club contact details, address etc. If your club grows successful you can then use your blog to add song sheets and news to for prospective members. Setting one of these up these days is childs play with very simple interfaces to get the basics in place in a very short space of time.

Finally, don't be afraid to ask for help in the wider ukulele community. I will certainly list any new ukulele club for free on the Got A Ukulele website and many other authors of uke sites will do the same if you ask them nicely. Ukulele discussion forums such as the excellent one on Ukulele Underground are also a great way for you to announce your club to the world.

Promotion is extremely hard work, and having like-minded friends to help will be a real boost. In fact having a friend who plays uke joining you will ensure you are not sat on your own on the first night!

ORGANISATION

How you run your club, it's structure, its style is entirely up to you and the members. What I would suggest though, is on your first night that you don't dictate or get hung up on structure too early. In fact, on your first night, it may be good to play very little ukulele and work out how you want the club to run first. Speak to your members, find out what they want, what they like to play, how frequently they want to meet and so on. Get those issues ironed out early and you will have happy members, but remember to hold regular review and feedback sessions with them!

New members are going to need music to play and as the organiser you need to make the first efforts in getting some chords and lyrics to simple songs with a broad appeal printed off. Please don't just steal someone else's hard work, try to create your own song sheets. With a bit of work on Word or another word processor you will soon have something that looks presentable and can be labeled as your own with a club name or logo. The easiest way to get these out to your membership is to email them well in advance, or you could be kind and print off a set of song sheets for everyone when they arrive. I highly recommend an A4 four ring binder containing plastic clear wallets to hold sheets. These allow songs to be moved about easily and the plastic stops them getting dog-eared.

Most importantly when it comes to organisation, YOU started the club, so YOU need to commit to it. You need to be the inspiration to ensure people come back again and again and that the numbers grow. Don't look bored (or worse not turn up without a prior apology) on the second meeting. As a club grows in size, others will offer to help and your admin burden will drop!

But those are just my thoughts. A successful club needs to be democratic and flexible. What suits one player doesn't necessarily suit another so listen to each other and work together. Most of all just get out there and play with others - it's hugely rewarding!

43. PORTABILITY IS THE THING

Without wishing to state the blindingly obvious, ukuleles are small. Compared to many musical instruments in fact, they are TINY. Not only does their size deliver their trademark sound, but also it brings another benefit and that is convenience and portability.

That benefit wasn't the key reason why I personally chose to play the ukulele, but it was certainly part of the decision making process. Having an instrument so small makes it extremely easy to just grab and take wherever you are going. If I am away on business that requires me staying away a night, I can sling a uke in the back of my car. In fact I've been known to be sat in a parking lot waiting for an appointment strumming my uke in the drivers seat - try that with a guitar! (And don't try it whilst driving..). They are easier to just grab when going to parties, to the pub, to the park. In fact they are so small there is really no reason not to take one with you everywhere. Think about it, what could be more fun on your holiday than strumming on a warm beach or round a campfire with friends? What could be more comforting when travelling alone than to have a uke with you in a lonely hotel room? I have many pals who take their ukes to work every day in order to have a strum on their lunch break. I often cycle with mine tucked in a rear pannier. Yes, the uke is the perfect travel companion.

So what do you want to consider if you want to travel more seriously with a ukulele? Well I suppose it depends on destination and means of travel. As mentioned in an earlier chapter, the standard soprano ukulele can easily be taken on an aircraft as hand luggage (though respectfully ask the chap you are sat next to before you start strumming mid flight!). A small soprano can also easily be strapped to, or inside, a rucksack if you are backpacking or camping.

If you are considering a more serious travel expedition, in particular, going somewhere more inhospitable (for that read hot / wet / muddy / sandy) you may want to consider leaving your solid, hand-made Koa uke at home and taking along something tougher and more suitable to the elements. An obvious choice for me would be the plastic backed Makala Dolphin, which my readers will know, is the instrument that I routinely recommend to beginners. They are not only tough as old boots, but also inexpensive enough that you won't mourn it too much if broken or stolen. A more serious uke alternative would be the Flea or Fluke ukes from the Magic Fluke Company. These instruments really are bombproof, yet give a really nice tone and are played by many professionals in live performances. Please don't try to test my theory, but I did once see mine tumble down a flight of stairs to sustain no damage apart from a slight ding on the headstock. More impressively, it was still in tune when I rescued it!

If you are doing any serious travelling, bear in mind that ukes are bound to pick up knocks and scratches along the way, and the tougher ukes will cope with these much better.

In addition, let me say a quick word about the ukuleles that are marketed as 'travel ukes'. These are made by some of the key ukulele brands and generally mean ukes with thinner bodies depth wise. I have personally never really understood these ukes for travel purposes. Don't get me wrong,

I've played both the Bruko and Kala models and they sound great, but being a half-inch thinner on the body seems to me like solving a problem that didn't exist in the first place. I don't find my existing ukes too bulky for travel, and the only benefit I can see to a thin uke is being able to slip it in a suitcase. No thank you, that to me seems a first class way of ensuring the uke is crushed in transit. And there is my gripe, whilst these ukes are thin; they are not tougher than any other wooden instrument in terms of construction or finish. Drop one and it may break as easily as a standard thickness uke. As such, for real travel, I'd prefer the tougher instruments I mentioned earlier, or an instrument that won't break the bank to replace.

So, you are now travelling your merry way around the world with your ukulele - what should you be particularly careful of? Well, several things really. If your uke gets wet make sure you wipe it down thoroughly and let it air dry. Never put it in a case wet if you can help it, and NEVER try to force it to dry by putting it somewhere hot (or applying a hair dryer!). Talking of hot places, hot temperatures plus ukulele equals bad news! Never leave your ukulele in a hot car or a hot tent or it will, frankly, break or fall apart! In some very hot environments you may also find the humidity is extremely low. If that is the case and you have an instrument with any solid wood in the construction, you might want to think about keeping it humidified and I deal with that in a later chapter in this book. Extremely humid climates are unlikely to damage an instrument in short bursts, but you may well find it plays havoc with your tuning! Don't forget to pack your tuner and a spare set of strings – how heartbreaking would it be to travel halfway around the world to a remote location, only to break a string on the first day!

Last but by no means least, you need to think about protection in the form of a good travelling case. These come in a variety of forms and you need to consider the appropriate trade off between weight / bulk and the level of protection you need. For some, a padded gig bag is enough, but if you are throwing a uke in and out of cars or holds on buses, you might want a hard case. A quick note again on flying - if you want to put your ukulele in the aircraft hold, a hard case is a minimum requirement, but be careful here too. Many hard cases are made from thin plywood and whilst they withstand knocks well, will not stand up to being stacked under a pile of suitcases, dropped from any height or thrown about by baggage handlers for fun. If you are going this route I would strongly recommend getting a high quality, ABS moulded case from a top brand like Hiscox or Calton. They are expensive but they work and will protect your investment.

So, what excuse is there NOT to travel with your ukulele companion? Give it a try and take that uke with you everywhere - its portability wins the day!

44. BASIC THEORY PT3 – 7th CHORDS

In earlier chapters in this book we looked at both Major and Minor Chords, and now we turn to 7th Chords to give you a little more variety in your playing.

A 7th chord is shown on chord sheets with a number 7 after the root note of the chord such as A7, C7 G7 etc. They are another important part of adding more feel to your music playing.

If you remember our basic chord theory for the major chords, we learned that a major chord was made up of the root, third of the root and fifth of the root notes from the major scale of the chord you are forming. The minor simply lowers the third of the root note down half a tone or a step. A major 7th chord simply adds another note that is a third above the root note.

On a ukulele this is usually achieved by taking the higher of the root notes and dropping it down two half tones.

If we take the C chord which is fingered 0003, we

learned in the chapter on Major chords that we have a C note on the open third string, and also a C note on the 1st string that you have fingered at the third fret. This second C note is also the higher of the two C notes in the chord, so if we drop that down two half tones (ie two frets) the chord fingering becomes 0001, and that plays you a C7!

Let us try that again with the A chord, which is fingered 2100. The two A notes we have created in that chord are on the fourth string at the second fret and the open first string which is naturally tuned to A. The highest note on a re-entrant tuned uke is actually the 4th string at the second fret, so we need to drop that one down two half tones (two frets) and that takes you to the nut. Therefore we play that string open and the fingering becomes 0100 - which is an A7 chord.

Turning to the G7 chord. A standard G chord is fingered 0232. In that chord we have a G note on the fourth string played open, and a G on the second string fingered at the third fret. That G on the second string is the highest, so If we drop that note down two half tones we get our G7 and the fingering would be 0212.

Why not try it with the other major chords, they work the same way!

45. THE ALL INCLUSIVE UKULELE

It never ceases to amaze me how diverse a crowd the ukulele community really is. We have people who play traditional music hall style uke and people who play rock or metal. We have folkies and we have jazzers. We have those who like to sensitively finger pick and those who enjoy nothing more than strumming out the latest pop songs in simple three-chord style. We have those who like to play alone, those who like to play in pairs or trios, all the way up to playing with dozens if not hundreds of other people. We have males and females, we have the young and we have the old. But the important thing is this - very few players I know are pigeon holed in just one area. In fact many players, including me, like to play in all sorts of styles - the uke really is that versatile and it draws out variety. You can also add to that, the fact you will often find players who prefer a certain style being totally welcoming of listening to or playing along with something outside their comfort zone. I'm not the world's biggest pop music fan, but what the heck; playing Jessie J's 'Price Tag' on a ukulele is FUN!

And what about skill levels? I have never made any bones about the fact that I am a mere average player. Sure, I talk a lot about the uke and made it my mission to help out players, beginners in particular, but my playing is just average. Rhythm and singing is my thing and I think my skill lies in getting a good chunky pattern going with a uke, but my fingerpicking leaves much to be desired. But again, a lot of uke players I know fall in to that category but still get such an enormous amount of pleasure from it. Sure there are the true modern ukulele greats out there who can create sounds with their ukes that leave me speechless - just check out anything by Jake Shimabukuro or James Hill if you want to see examples, but few reach those heights (not that one shouldn't try!). In my experience though, I have jammed ukulele with friends many times, often in front of an audience - some players are more accomplished than I am, and some players are just starting out, capable of only two or three simple chords and still struggling with sore fingers and how to strum naturally. Yet, when I'm playing and look around, not only do I see happy listeners, but I see happy players too. From the accomplished to the struggling, everyone has a smile on his or her face. Take a look for yourself, join a jam or a club and you will see the very same thing. And in clubs around the world I am sure you will see it too. There is no one-upmanship or snobbery in the ukulele world and masters of the instrument will find themselves happily playing along with beginners and vice versa.

And of course we can't ignore the price. Yes, there are some extremely poor quality cheap instruments on the market from makers jumping on the rise of the ukulele in recent times, but if you buy from a reputable dealer, one can start with ukulele for about £25 a £30. I know because I own one. I have had as many happy times playing a cheap Makala Dolphin with friends as I have playing a mid priced Mainland uke or an expensive handmade Koa Kanile'a or Koaloha uke. I'm not going to insult your intelligence, of course the higher end instruments DO sound better and so they should, but that doesn't mean a player with a cheap uke is unable to have fun jamming with friends playing instruments that cost hundreds of pounds more. I still pick up my Makala regularly and would have no qualms taking it to a local uke jam. Name me another instrument that suits so many budgets?

So there you have three good examples that show the all-inclusive nature of the ukulele. When you start to play one you join a worldwide community that is only too happy to help regardless of your ability, your music tastes or your choice of instrument.

But I will end with a subtler example that demonstrates the uke as being an inclusive instrument. When I was going through my first stages of school we were forced to play the recorder as a class instrument. I despised it, which was really contrary to what I have always enjoyed all my life – music. For me though I just didn't like it. I've since read a variety of theories as to why the Government chose to push it in schools, such as price and it supposedly helping kids get along with piano notation. Sadly, not that many kids in modern times have families with the funds to support buying a piano, or even to pay for lessons, but my gripe with the recorder was that it was stuck in your mouth (obviously!). Nobody can sing while playing it, and for children, singing is a fun activity that

EVERYONE can join in with, and what I really liked best about music class at school. So, if you are the child, like I was, with a dislike for the recorder, you are stuck with it no matter how hard or boring you are finding it. You turn up to group classes and feel you can't really offer anything. Now take the ukulele, which is being introduced to junior children in some schools in the UK now, as it has been in Canada for many years. It is cheap for parents to buy like the recorder, but bear in mind that there is no way all children will enjoy it or will progress equally, also like the recorder. Some will struggle, BUT it's not stuck in their mouths! When a teaching class then introduces singing together with ukulele, the whole class can come together with very mixed abilities, but still take part. I recently discussed this very subject with a music teacher and that is exactly what they found in class. Some children struggled to get up to speed with the ukulele, but made up for it by singing, some liked strumming but sang less and of course there was a whole spectrum in-between. A class came together as one with everybody contributing and improving together.

That's the all-inclusive ukulele for you.

46. HUMIDITY

When you are starting out with your ukulele you may read references and warnings about humidity and how it can affect your uke. What do you need to know?

Humidity is a natural part of the atmosphere, and with changes in seasons and the weather; humidity also changes all around us. It refers to how much moisture there is in the air around us, and when humidity levels are at the extremes, it can cause issues with your instrument, some very serious. It should be borne in mind that this issue mainly affects solid wood instruments and less so ukuleles made from laminated wood, which are naturally stronger and less prone to warping. Wood is a natural breathing material and it changes naturally over time by expanding and contracting as it takes on or loses moisture from the air around it. Severe changes in what the wood is used to can have disastrous effects.

If you lose moisture in the air (low humidity or arid climates) there is a risk of the fingerboard or body shrinking slightly, and the instrument possibly cracking, splitting or distorting if left unchecked for too long a period of time. Too much humidity and you can find the top of the instrument swelling and similar distortions occurring although thankfully it may be unlikely to crack. At the very best this can cause cosmetic issues with the ukulele (such as small cracks in the finish or the wood itself), but at worst can throw the instrument permanently out or destroy it.

Before you start to panic though, the requirement to keep a check on humidity only applies to those of you with instruments in locations with humidity at either extreme (those in the Far East, or Arizona, take note.)

The best humidity for a wooden instrument is considered to be between 45% and 55%. If you have a humidity gauge in your home and are regularly falling way below or above this level you should think about your options.

In a dry climate, you may want to consider investing in a humidifier – this is a small device that lives in the ukulele case, or hangs inside the sound hole that contains a sponge material that holds distilled water. The water is then given off through evaporation and keeps the instrument in a more humid atmosphere. Ensure you purchase a product designed for the ukulele, as you need to ensure it maintains that ideal humidity level. I stress that this is only required in a very dry environment, and if your uke doesn't need moisture; forcing humid air onto it can damage the instrument permanently!

If you live in a very humid country, then your problem is tougher to solve and you may need to consider a de-humidifier for the room your ukulele is kept in. A tightly sealed case may help, but keep a close eye on the instrument.

For those who live in more stable climates, be aware that you can create your own problems too - never leave a ukulele next to a radiator or heater, in direct sunlight or in a hot car! Houses with a central heating system that runs like a steam train and keeps a house hot hot hot, may also create dry and damaging environments, and you may want to think about a humidifier (or move the uke into a room that isn't kept at temperatures like the Sahara Desert...)

Humidity gauges are cheap and easily found online - if you think you may have an issue with your local environment I would urge you to buy one and consider your options as if left unchecked in the long term your instrument could literally fall apart.

47. MORE ADVANCED BUILDING TECHNIQUES

Earlier we looked at the more common ukulele shapes, sizes and woods, but as you explore the world of the uke, you will no doubt come across many less common techniques that are used in building these instruments. In the main, most ukes follow a fairly standard pattern in their build, which makes them look like miniature Spanish guitars. Many brands to try to play around with the shape, and of course there are pineapples and boat paddles and many others But as new builders come on the scene looking to spruce the world of the uke up, they are increasingly looking beyond the shape of the instrument and into other options that give a ukulele a certain something different.

THE ZERO FRET

On the majority of ukuleles, the strings run between two key points, the bridge and the nut, at tension. The distance between the two of these is called the scale length and that distance needs to be exactly right in relation to the fret spacing to allow the ukulele to play in tune all over the fingerboard.

Some players have problems with this tuning (called Intonation) and it often stems from this distance being inaccurately set. When you look at a ukulele nut, they are usually quite a lot wider than a fret, and the string sits in a slot cut in that nut. A well-cut nut will have a "break" point within that slot which represents the exact point at which the string is held in tension down the neck to the bridge. If that point is cut badly, meaning to far one way or the other, intonation down the neck may be an issue.

The 'zero fret' was originally introduced in guitar making as a cost saving exercise to make up for shoddy nuts. All it is is another fret wire placed immediately next to the actual nut (on the string side), set at a position where this represents the correct distance from the bridge for the scale length. Therefore, the nut itself is purely there for holding the strings in the right spacing, but the zero fret holds the string at the correct length and height. As such it actually creates a way of eliminating accuracy issues at the nut end of the instrument.

Some claim that the downside is that you lose a bit of the ring and sustain from playing open strings, as each string now will naturally sound like it is being fretted even when open, but I suspect that is subjective.

If you have seen a Flea or Fluke ukulele up close, you will see that they employ the zero fret and that is one of the reasons why they are a trouble free instrument when it comes to action and intonation.

SHAPED SOUND HOLES

Not all sound holes need to be round! Round is certainly the most common, quite simply because it is the easiest (and cheapest) to cut, but we are increasingly seeing variations on this, some very imaginatively!

Koaloha ukuleles use a patented shape on their sound holes, which looks like a very rounded triangle, and they have patented this shape and called it the "Musubi". Does it change the sound of my Koaloha ukulele? Impossible to say, but it looks nice, and people do point it out and say, "that's different!".

Other brands use the sound hole shape to reflect their names, the most obvious example being the Eddie Finn range of ukuleles which have a sound hole in the shape of a sharks fin!

You may also have seen the Ovation Applause model ukes that take their design from their guitar big brothers and feature off centre, smaller sound holes within the leaf decoration that these ukes and guitars are famous for.

Finally a big thumbs up to the UK Luthier Darryl Cursley of Cursley Ukuleles, who crafted a beautiful tenor uke for his wife with an intricate sound hole in the shape of a butterfly. It really is quite stunning and you can find pictures on Got A Ukulele and the Cursley Ukulele website.

PERSONAL SOUND HOLES

This is an intriguing idea, though not something I have played myself. A personal sound hole is an additional hole (or holes) cut in the side of the instrument on the side that faces the ceiling and the players face. The idea is that the hole helps project the sound of the uke to the actual player as well as the audience allowing for a more pleasing playing experience and a better idea for the players as to the sound that is being projected.

Riptide ukuleles employ this design, and this feature is increasingly being offered as an option on bespoke ukuleles such as those made by Moore Bettah and Lichty.

FLUSH FINGERBOARDS

On the majority of ukuleles you see, the fingerboard is usually another thin piece of wood that is glued on to the wood of the neck and as such it sits a little higher by a couple of millimetres) than the top of the instrument itself.

In fact, that tradition is a relatively new technique borrowed from the world of guitar making to provide for prettier woods on the ukulele fingerboard (rosewood and ebony for example), which are less suitable for crafting the actual neck itself. In the depths of ukulele building history however, luthiers would avoid this altogether and actually set the frets directly into the top of the neck wood itself, meaning that the end of the fingerboard ran flush with the top of the instrument.

One or two modern day ukes employ this feature and at one time I owned a slimline Bruko ukulele that was built this way. It brings about two key changes over a normal fingerboard. Firstly the strings are a lot closer to the body of the instrument, which I found made strumming easier (though less so, picking) as fingers were less likely to be 'caught' by the strings. It also allowed for some clever use of the top of the instrument for "fretting" notes beyond the end of the fingerboard into really high pitch territory!

There are probably countless other ideas that builders are now trying out, in order to create something special in the marketplace too. There are carbon fibre ukes, plastic ukes (completely made of plastic, not just plastic backs!), ukes made of strips of laminated bamboo, uke / banjo / zither hybrids, five string ukes, guitarleles and many more.

What unusual designs and features have you come across?

48. BUILDING A UKULELE WORKFLOW

Please accept my apologies in advance of this chapter for using the word 'workflow'. I think it is clumsy and relates better to those in the IT world, but bear with me! I wanted to write a chapter about getting into your stride when it comes to ukulele practice in a more ordered and efficient way.

Workflow is a term often relating to a structured approach to working through tasks to get the job done in the most efficient and productive way. I suppose that can also apply to ukulele practice sessions, and anything that helps people get their practice into a shape that makes for better learning and progression has to be a good thing. It is a simple fact though, many people who get their very first ukulele approach learning and practice in a more haphazard manner and as a result become frustrated and quit.

So I am writing this for those of you who have mastered the key chords, and can strum fairly comfortably and are now looking to move on to develop your skills. To do that you will need to dedicate time to practice and there are no short cuts. Perhaps you've mastered a song or two, but want to push on. Earlier we looked at many tips on how to go about practicing, so this is written to accompany that chapter, as a general guide to structuring your practice, not telling you WHAT to practice. You can fill your time with what feels comfortable to you, perhaps just technique, song learning, theory, or whatever. If you want to practice all three, all I'd say is keep it balanced. Too much of anything may well frustrate you!

HOME PRACTICE

Most of your ukulele practice when you are starting out may well be undertaken at home, and perhaps alone. It may well follow on from playing with others the night or day before, but more on that later. As such you need to work on some self-discipline and planning before you get stuck in.

Firstly, think about setting yourself some goals and sticking to them. The key here is not to set challenges too high, too fast. It's always tempting to want to immediately play a favourite but very complicated song on day one, but that may be too much of a challenge for you as a beginner. Collect some song sheets that you feel are just a little bit ahead of your current ability, but not too far, and try to stick with those until you master the ability to play them as perfectly (or as good as you can get!) before moving on.

There are no hard and fast rules on how much to practice the uke, when, or what you do in your practice session. Obviously too little practice will slow your progress to a point that you don't actually see any progression at all and conversely too much could actually start to work counter productively. You need to find the right balance.

Try to set your challenges or goals to be interesting, refreshing and achievable. By way of an example, let's say you want to learn two new uke songs in your week ahead. You could make a practice plan as follows:

Day 1 - warm up, strum practice, practice song 1, general strum practice, finish.

Day 2 - warm up, fingerpicking practice, practice song 2, finger stretching exercise, practice song 2, theory, finish.

Day 3 - warm up, strum practice, finger stretching, practice song 1, practice song 2, finish.

And so on, filling the days and keeping your sessions varied and interesting whilst always keeping a regular eye on the goals you have set.

Now that may come across all a bit rigid, and I'm not a big fan of rigid teaching. I don't expect you to need to write a physical plan and stick it on your fridge door, and leave copies around the house. What I am saying is to keep a check on what you are doing on a daily basis, what you are missing out on and try to keep an efficient balance going forward. You may find that some things come to you naturally and therefore you can practice those a little less. Some things may be a struggle and you may need to devote more time to those. Likewise you will find elements that you don't particularly enjoy but recognise they are important (theory, for example is the area I dread reading about) – so make sure you don't avoid it altogether, but equally don't pile those elements on to the point that it stops being enjoyable. Keep it fun, but keep an eye on what you are doing. I've seen many beginners practicing week by week not keeping watch, and getting a little entrenched in, say, just one song, that they are missing out on some basic skills that they need to find the time to move on to other styles. By keeping it more balanced, your progress should be more efficient.

PLAYING WITH OTHERS

As I've said many times, I highly, highly recommend new players try to play with others as much as possible, either with friends, or better still, a uke club or jamming session. This way of practicing really does help players improve ukulele skills at a fast rate. It's down to the mix of being able to see and others play, with a bit of competition thrown in!

But of course, you can't be playing uke with friends all the time, every day. Many ukulele clubs only meet once a week or less, so you need to find a way of extending and working on your experiences with your club to fit in to your general home practice. I suppose you could join more than one club if you are lucky enough to live in an area with many around you but for most people that is unlikely to be possible.

Most good ukulele clubs offer song sheets for the club to learn and play along to, distributed either by hard copy, by email or via download. Make sure you keep these and concentrate on the songs the club is working on at that time. You may feel restricted if the songs in one week are not your cup of tea, but stick with it. The important thing is that you try to learn to play with others, and there isn't much point you doggedly learning "The Green Green Grass Of Home" when the club don't play that song. Sure, find the time to learn it alongside the club songs, but don't get bogged down. (Serious point, if you are planning on learning that song and introducing it at a uke club, you are braver than I am..)

One 'Got A Ukulele' reader emailed me recently asking about getting audio files on the site as he struggled to remember how some songs went after returning from a club session. I've avoided doing that for copyright reasons, but he raised a very good point and there are answers to that. In the simplest sense many modern mobiles offer voice recording so you could always record some songs whilst the group play to help remind you during home practice sessions. There are also some excellent audio recorders on the market that record to SD memory cards, such as the Zoom H2 which I use. These pick up recordings in very high quality via 360 degree microphones so you really can get that club sound when you get home - just ask permission first! Your other alternative is to buy the original music of course. Either way, that is a really good part of your ukulele practice workflow - learning to listen. If you are practicing a new song, do make sure you have access to the song you are playing in audio format. There is nothing tougher than a beginner trying to learn a song they only half know from a set of words and chords on a sheet of paper! There is also nothing worse than being in the audience at a ukulele jam session and hearing the group hit the chorus of a particular song, stop, then say, "oh, I don't know how this bit goes.."

Fit your club songs into your home practice and again, keep it balanced.

Always remember, listen to your head and your fingers. If you are getting frustrated or sore, take a break and don't fight it. Most of all, keep your practicing plans fresh and interesting and don't get bogged down.

What are your practicing tips and routines? I'd love to hear them!

49. MOVING ONWARDS

So, you bought your first ukulele and I hope that having read this far that you are getting on well with it (if you are not, why not? What has the humble uke ever done to you??). I hope that you are now giving some thought to getting out there and playing with others, being more adventurous with your uke, and building some structure into how you choose to practice.

So how about I sum this book up with some resolutions you can set for your ukulele year ahead?

Let's get one thing out of the way - this is not going to be a list of the obvious resolutions you may hear elsewhere - you know the sort of thing - "learn chords XYZ, learn ten songs, learn some scales, practice every week", that kind of thing. If you seriously want to progress with the uke, those really should be a given in any case. These are just easy to achieve, less 'material' things, some of which have been described in this book. If you have read this far, bookmark this chapter and come back to it to see how you are getting on.

PLAY WITH OTHER PEOPLE

You are probably tired of hearing me say this, but playing with or for others is one of the best ways to progress and expand horizons on the uke. Playing with others builds confidence, creates new ideas, and generally just helps you progress quicker. Grab a friend with a uke, grab a friend without a uke and ask them to buy one, whatever, just grab somebody! Then sit down and start playing together alongside your normal practice. Better still, grab said friend and do the next thing below!

JOIN A CLUB

Wow - it really staggers me how many ukulele clubs and societies there must be out there, and whilst the listing on Got A Ukulele is big, I suspect it only scratches the surface. As a blogger on that site I have also seen a huge increase in email requests telling me about new clubs, so I very much hope that if there isn't a ukulele club in your local area today, that there may be in due course. If you have the opportunity to visit a local club regularly I would strongly advise it. Meet with like-minded players, both beginners and experienced alike, and share ideas and play together. This will give your playing a HUGE boost. No ukulele club nearby? Set one up!

DEVELOP YOUR STYLES

You have a whole year ahead of you, and there is no need to rush, but if you are an absolute beginner, you will soon find yourself in something of a rut of playing up down basic strumming. Start to experiment, work on some rhythm and syncopation with your strumming, or try working on some slow finger picking of your favourite songs. Don't be afraid to try playing a style of music that you ordinarily don't listen to – you may be surprised how well it works on the ukulele (trust me – Gloria Gaynors 'I Will Survive' works surprisingly well!). Whatever you choose, don't be rigid in your learning, don't rely on strum patterns as the be all and end all - learn your instrument, and learn to understand what it can do for you and by you. There is no right and wrong (within certain limits), and you need to work to make your instrument become one with you. Experiment!

MAKE A VIDEO

I gave you my reasons for doing this in an earlier chapter. Over the last couple of years I have seen so many ukulele players online who have drummed up the courage to record their tracks and put them on YouTube for others to comment on. The ukulele community is a great, friendly place, and in the vast majority of cases I have seen nothing but constructive support for those who are prepared to share their playing in public. It's less scary than playing to an audience, but can reap better rewards in terms of direct feedback. I've seen players I know go on from YouTube to playing live for money and getting record deals. I'd strongly recommend the Ukulele Underground site forum and checking the videos section for examples of what people are posting. Sure you will see some advanced stuff that may seem beyond your current abilities, but that community welcomes absolute beginner videos also. And of course, if you want my own opinion on any video you record, just send me the link. If I really like it I will put it up on Got A Ukulele and give it more exposure!

TRY SOME OTHER UKES

I apologise in advance about this suggestion, but if the ukulele bug bites, you WILL be buying another before long. It is what is commonly known in ukulele player circles as UAS (Ukulele Acquisition Syndrome) and you may already have it. I've been suffering from it for years.. I know that at the present time budgets are tight for many people but if you can manage it, don't be afraid to try a new ukulele size alongside the one you have. If that isn't possible, experiment with alternate tunings for your instrument, and in particular if you have larger sized uke, consider playing with the Low G tuning as opposed to the more common re-entrant style discussed earlier in this book.

But most of all (and this isn't an idea or a resolution) just have the most fun you can possibly have. The ukulele is a happy, social instrument. Take it everywhere with you, learn it, explore it, but have fun.

Here's to your ukulele year ahead, and I hope that this book and my encouragement means that in another years time many of you are making even greater strides with the humble uke. Best of luck to you all

50. UKULELE INSPIRATION LIST

I have included this as a kind of appendix to the book. A while ago on Got A Ukulele I ran a competition where to enter, you told me your favourite three songs to play on the ukulele. There were lots of entries!

A common question new players ask me is to give them some suggestions for songs to play. Well I can go better – I can give you suggestions of LOTS of songs to play on the ukulele drawn from uke players around the world. You may not know or even like all of them but this list of entries to that competition is extensive and I would challenge you to find a song or two on here that doesn't spark some interest.

So with thanks to all my readers, here is the complete inspiration list. You shouldn't have too much trouble finding the lyrics and chords to these songs on the internet, and they are all playable on the uke as the suggestions come from actual players.

Enjoy!

1234

Aint She Sweet

All My Loving – Beatles

All Of Me

Always Look On The Bright Side Of Life – Monty Python

Anyone Else But You – Moldy Peaches

Ask – The Smiths

April May – Peter Berryman

Auld Lang Syne

Autumn Leaves

Bad Moon Rising – Creedence Clearwater Revival

Banana Pancakes

Bei Mir Bist Du Schoen

Better Together- Jack Johnson

All I Got- Newton Faulkner

Greensleeves

Beverley Hills Cop Theme – Harald Faltermayer

Big Strong Girl – Deb Talan

Birdhouse In Your Soul – They Might Be Giants

Blister In The Sun – Violent Femmes

Blowing In The Wind – Bob Dylan

Blue Monk-Thelonious Monk

Hey Soul Sister-Train

Blue Moon

Blue Moon Of Kentucky

Breakdown – Tom Petty

Brown Sugar – Rolling Stones

Build Me Up Buttercup – The Foundations

Charleston – James P Johnston

Christmas Cookies – George Strait

Clair de Lune- Debussy

Fast Car - Tracy Chapman

The Scientist - Coldplay

Classico – Tenacious D

Clementine

Comets – Cocoon

Creep – Radiohead

Don't Think Twice, it's Alright - Bob Dylan

Sugar Baby - Bob Dylan

I Believe in You - Bob Dylan

Dont Dream It's Over – Crowded House

Dont Get Around Much Anymore

Dream Police- Cheap Trick

Drop Baby Drop

Drop Baby/Honey Baby - Manao Company/Three Plus

I Hear Music - Kaau Crater Boys

Jammin - Bob Marley

Easy Like Sunday Morning – the Commordores

Eight Days A Week – Beatles

Eku U Morning Dew

Faith – George Michael

First Day Of My Life - Bright Eyes

First Impressions

Fishermans Blues – The Waterboys

Five Foot Two

Freebird – Lynyrd Skynyrd

Froggie Went A Courtin'

Fur Elise

Ghost Riders In The Sky – Johnny Cash

Girl from Ipanema - Astrud Gilberto and Stan Get

Summer Wind - Frank Sinatra

Eggplant - Michael Franks

Haele

Hallelujah – Leonard Cohen

Harder Better Faster Stronger – Daft Punk

Harry Potter Theme

Hene

Hey Soul Sister – Train

Hey There Delilah – Plain White T's

Hotel California – Eagles

House Of The Rising Sun – The Animals

How Deep Is Your Love - Bee Gees

Karma Cameleon - Culture Club

Jolly Holiday - from Mary Poppins

I Gotta Feeling – Black Eyed Peas

I Shot The Sherriff – Bob Marley

I Wanna Be Like You

I Will Survive -Gloria Gaynor

I'll Never Find Another You – The Seekers

I'll See You In My Dreams

I'm Satisfied With My Gal

I'm Yours – Jason Mraz

Into The Mystic – Van Morrisson

Jackson – Johnny Cash

Just A Gigolo – David Lee Roth

Kaulana Kawaihae

Kids – MGMT

Kill The Director – The Wombats

Last Thing On My Mind

Leaning On A Lamppost – George Formby

Leroy Brown – Jim Croce

Let It Be- Beatles

Little Brown Jug

Little Lion Man – Mumford and Sons

Louie Louie – The Kingsmen

Mad World – Tears For Fears

Magic Martian Ukulele Waltz

Maire's Wedding

Man On The Flying Trapeze – Ukulele Ike

Moondance – Van Morrisson

Moonglow

Meditação

Music Box Waltz

Mull Of Kintyre – Wings

Na Moku Eha

No Rain – Blind Melon

Oh Dear - Brandi Carlile

Oh Mary Don't You Weep

Oh Mother, What'll I Do Now – George Formby

Oh, It's Love

On The Radio - Regina Spektor

House Of The Rising Sun - the animals

Once More For The Road

One Note Samba - Carlos Jobim

Tanta Til Beate - Lillebjorn Nilsen

Leaning On A Lamp Post - Noel Grey

Only Love Can Break Your Heart – Neil Young

Over The Rainbow

Overseas Stomp

Penas do tiê

Perhaps, Perhaps, Perhaps

Postcards From Italy – Beirut

Pretty When It's New – Merle Haggard

Pricetag – Jessie J

Puff The Magic Dragon – Peter, Paul and Mary

Put Your Records On – Corrine Bailey Rae

Rawhide

Rhythm Of Love – Plain White T's

Rise Up – Eddie Vedder

Romanesca Guardame Las Vacas for 4-course renaissance guitar – Alonso Mudarra

Sabor a Mi

San Francisco Bay Blues-Eric Clapton

La Isla Bonita - Madonna

Ain't She Sweet

Saturday In The Park – Chicago

Scarlet Tide – Elvis Costello

Sentimental Heart – She and Him

Shaving Cream

She Thinks My Tractor's Sexy

Silence Kit – Pavement

Sitting On The Dock Of The Bay – Otis Redding

Skullcrusher Mountain

Sleigh Bells – U900

Something - the Beatles

Strawberry Fields Forever - The Beatles

Down By The Riverside - Traditional

Something – Beatles

Speak Now- Taylor Swift

Perfect- Pink

Listen to the Rain- Evanescence

Knock Three Times On The Ceiling If You Want Me

Stairway To Heaven – Led Zeppelin

Stand By Me – Ben E King

Stardust

Starry Eyed – Ellie Goulding

Sugar Magnolia – Grateful Dead

Sunny Afternoon – The Kinks

Tears In Heaven – Eric Clapton

The Cover Of The Rolling Stone

The Cowboy Song

The General – Dispatch

The Hypnotist - Craig Robertson

When I'm 64 – Beatles

There She Goes – The La's

Three Little Birds – Bob Marley

Thunder Road – Bruce Springsteen

Time After Time – Cyndi Lauper

To Make You Feel My Love – Bob Dylan

Tomorrow Is A Long Time – Bob Dylan

Tonight You Belong To Me

Ukulele Waltz- Aldrine Guerrero

Under African Skies – Paul Simon

Valentine – Kina Grannis

Vampire – Juno Soundtrack

Venus

Viva La Vida – Coldplay

Watching the Wheels -John Lennon

Opihi Man - Ka'au Crater Boys version

Sugar Magnolia - Grateful Dead

When I'm Cleaning Windows

While My Guitar Gently Weeps – Beatles

Wild Mountain Thyme

Wish You Were Here – Pink Floyd

Wonderful Tonight – Eric Clapton

Yellow Bird

Yesterday – Beatles

Yoshimi Battles the Pink Robots - The Flaming Lips

Telephone - Lady GaGa

You and I – Ingrid Michaelson

You Are My Sunshine

You Belong To Me (from the soundtrack of Shrek)

Let it Be - The Beatles

In My Life - The Beatles

You Ruined Everything – Jonathan Coulton

You've Got A Friend In Me – Randy Newman

51. UKULELE REFERENCE

So, we have come a long way and covered a lot of ground. I hope I have been able to steer you in the right direction on many topics connected with the ukulele, and I hope you feel a little more empowered rather than restricted. This book is only part of the process, your practice is critical, as is making use of the many other wonderful resources available out there. Join a club, go to a tutor, heck, start your own club!

To finish, and before I provide you with a handy ukulele glossary, I thought it would be worthwhile sharing with you a list of resources that I think are helpful to the beginner.

Got A Ukulele – http://www.gotaukulele.com - My site – had to be on the list really didn't it? Keep an eye on that blog as I provide chord charts, song sheets, and reviews of instruments and accessories.

UkuleleUnderground – http://www.ukuleleunderground.com – In my opinion, one of the best ukulele resources on the internet. The video lessons and tuition on the main site are second to none, but most useful of all is the forum. Sign up and come and say hi! The people on the UU forum are some of the friendliest you will meet and you should not be afraid to ask a silly question.

Get Tuned – http://www.get-tuned.com – a simple site that provides a usable online ukulele tuner if you don't have one of your own.

Ukulele Hunt – http://ukulelehunt.com – A superb ukulele blog with a massive amount of song tips, videos, and even more ebooks to download.

Aside from those, Google is your friend. You will find a wealth of ukulele advice on the Internet. YouTube is a real revelation in my mind to anyone playing a musical instrument, quite simply because of the huge amount of videos out there of real people playing. The perfect place to hone your technique and skill.

Good luck!

GLOSSARY

Action

The height of the strings relative to the fingerboard. High action is both difficult to play and can cause tuning issues. Conversely, if your action is too low, you may find the strings buzz on the frets.

Aquila

Italian string brand who use a patented artificial gut substitute called Nylgut. Considered by many to be the best all round ukulele string, and they can bring great results with beginner instruments.

Back

The back of the ukulele, with the sound hole facing the floor, this refers to the single piece of wood that makes up the rear face of the instrument.

Baritone

The largest scale of ukulele (19 inches) developed in the 1940's and usually tuned DGBE

Barre

The action of placing a finger (usually the forefinger) across all strings of the ukulele at a certain fret to effect the action of moving the nut down, and shortening the strings. This allows for chords to be played at a higher register.

Binding

The term given to a cosmetic finish applied around the edges of the ukulele body (where the top and back meet the sides) usually in a contrasting colour and used to hide the join between the woods. Binding is also common along the edges of the fingerboard. It is not essential and only employed to add to the attractiveness of the instrument.

Bridge

The wooden piece glued on the top of the ukulele below the sound hole which usually holds the saddle. The strings pass over the saddle and this acts as the end point for the vibrating end of the string. Some ukuleles have a one piece bridge without a saddle, where the saddle is moulded into the bridge itself. The term bridge has become common place for that part of the ukulele.

Capo

A device which attaches to the ukulele at a certain fret which, when tightened, has the effect of moving the nut to that fret, thus shortening the strings and raising the register of the instrument. Usually used by those wishing to play the same chord patterns to a song that is otherwise to deep for them to comfortably sing to.

Chord

A combination of notes played in harmony, usually effected on a ukulele by holding strings at different frets allowing the individual strings to play complimentary notes.

Chord Chart

A diagram showing a range of chords and how the fingers should be applied to the strings (and at which frets) to play the particular chord.

Chord Progression

A sequence of chords played one after each other.

Concert

The size up from a Soprano Ukulele allowing slightly easier fingering, usually tuned GCEA and with a 15" Scale Length.

Fingerboard

The area of the neck over which the strings run and into which the frets are mounted. The fingerboard is where your fretting hand holds the notes by pressing down on the strings between the frets. Fingerboards are often made out of a strip of dark wood or dark stained wood applied to the neck of the ukulele.

Fingerstyle

The technique of playing the ukulele by picking individual strings with the fingers or a pick, rather than strumming them.

Flea and Fluke

Names of modern designed ukuleles with distinctive shapes and moulded plastic backs. Their design is exact and are rarely badly set up. Manufactured by the Magic Fluke Company in the USA.

Flat

A note that is sounded below its usual pitch – refers to a note that is deeper.

Fret

The thin strips of metal set into the neck of a ukulele to allow you to change notes. By holding a string between frets, the fret nearest the bridge acts as a nut and shortens the length of the string, hence sharpening the note higher.

Fretting

The action of placing a finger between frets, thus changing the length and pitch of the string.

Gig /Gigging

Playing a live show

Hardware

The term used to describe the parts on a ukulele, most commonly the strap buttons, any electronics, the tuners etc.

Harmony

Two or more notes sounding simultaneously.

Headstock

The flat piece of wood at the end of the neck that holds the tuning pegs

Inlay

The name given to the fret markers on the ukulele fingerboard. Most commonly simply white dots, but often can be styled into other shapes or patterns on more expensive instruments. Beginner instrument inlays are usually made of plastic, but more expensive ukuleles have inlays made of mother of pearl or a similar substance.

Neck

The piece of wood that holds the fingerboard, and runs between the Body of the ukulele and the Headstock.

Nut

The strip of material, either hard plastic or bone located at the top end of the fingerboard over which the strings are held in slots on their way to the tuning pegs. The accurate placement of the nut in relation to the saddle is essential for accurate tuning.

Peghead

See Headstock

Saddle

The thin strip of material housed in the bridge over which the strings run, holding them at the right length for the ukulele to play accurately. (See also, Bridge)

Scale Length

The distance between the Nut and the Saddle, for which accuracy is essential if the ukulele is to play in tune.

Setup

The process of adjusting the action and other parts of a ukulele to provide the optimum playing characteristics.

Sharp

The term given to a note that is sounded higher than its normal pitch.

Soprano

The smallest of the standard ukulele types, usually tuned GCEA and with a scale length of 13".

Sound hole

The open hole in the Top of the ukulele, that projects the sound of the instrument.

Strumming

The action of running fingers or a pick over all of the strings, in an up and down motion whilst a chord is held.

Tablature / Tabs

A system of notation, alternative to sheet music, for educating a player in the performance of a piece of music.

Tenor

The second largest in the standard ukulele family, usually tuned GCEA or DGBE and with a 17" Scale

Length.

Top

The term given to the flat top of the body of the ukulele that holds the Bridge and the Sound Hole

Tuners

The pegs (either geared or held by friction) attached to the Headstock of the ukulele, the turning of which tightens or loosens the strings allowing them to be tuned to pitch.

THANKS AND ACKNOWLEDGEMENTS

Over the last few years a number of people have given me a huge amount of support in respect of the Got A Ukulele site and the books I released. A number of people have also inspired me through their playing and performing and to those I am also thankful.

With that in mind, and in no particular order, I'd recommend that any ukulele player checks out the names on the list below as I am sure you will find something from them that appeals, be they a player, a writer or a uke maker. I know some of them well, some of them not at all, but I've seen their work.

Thanks!

Lori Apthorp at Uke Leash

Alan Okami at Koaloha Ukuleles

Rae Carter

Darryl Cursley – Cursley Ukuleles

Mike Hater at Mainland Ukuleles

Ken Middleton

Tricity Vogue

Liz Panton

All of the gang at Godalming UkeJam including Penny Fazackerley, Adam Wolters, Tim Wakeham, Claire Turner, Lee and Stephanie Evans.

Joey Paul

Kim Ruohio

Alastair Wood of Ukulele Hunt

Lorraine Bow

Matthew Gunning at Balham Ukulele Society

James Hill

Bosko & Honey

Aldrine Guererro

Kyle Frazer

Liz Quilty

Jessica Latshaw

Patrick at Musique83

Nigel Thornbury at Highly Strung

Jake Shimabukuro

Amanda Palmer

Paul Tucker at Southern Ukulele Store

Ukulele Mike

Eddie Vedder

Randy Chang

The Nantwich N'Ukes

And anyone else who has tweeted, contributed or read!

ALSO BY BARRY MAZ

What Ukulele Players Really Want To Know
More Of What Ukulele Players Really Want To Know
Chords That Ukulele Players Really Want To Know

Available on Kindle, Nook, Kobo, iBooks, Sony and in paperback.